CHILDREN'S HUMOR

CHILDREN'S HUMOR

A PSYCHOLOGICAL ANALYSIS

by Martha Wolfenstein

FOREWORD BY ALAN DUNDES

Indiana University Press

Bloomington & London

ACKNOWLEDGMENTS

IT IS pleasant to recall in connection with this study the stimulating discussions and valuable suggestions of Elaine and Daniel Bell, Jean Bram, Berta Bornstein, Marjorie and Irving Janis, Ernst Kris, Nathan Leites, Margaret Mead, and Evelyn and David Riesman. I am also warmly grateful to the schools that so kindly provided the possibility for my observations and interviews—and especially to the children who told me their jokes.

I am greatly obliged to the International Universities Press for permission to include in this book my paper on "Children's Understanding of Jokes," which appeared in *The Psychoanalytic Study of the Child,* Volume VIII.

Indiana University Press edition published 1978 by arrangement with The Free Press, a division of Macmillan Publishing Co., Inc.

Manufactured in the United States of America
cl ISBN 0-253-31351-1   pa ISBN 0-253-20206-X   LC 77-15760

Contents

FOREWORD

Martha Wolfenstein (1911-1976) was a specialist in clinical child psychology and a respected practitioner of child therapy. After receiving her doctorate from Radcliffe in 1939 and teaching psychology at Hunter College from 1943 to 1947, she was associated with Ruth Benedict and Margaret Mead at Columbia University on a research project in contemporary cultures from 1947 to 1950. In 1950, she co-authored with Nathan Leites, who was at that time her husband, a book entitled *Movies: A Psychological Sketch*. Throughout her career Martha Wolfenstein continued to be interested in all sorts of fantasy ranging from children's art to motion pictures.

In 1959, Wolfenstein joined the department of psychiatry at the Albert Einstein College of Medicine at Yeshiva University where she remained until her death. However, it was her earlier experience as a psychological consultant or staff psychiatrist at several New York City private schools which provided most of the data and insights which led to *Children's Humor*. Although a few parts of the work had appeared in article form in *The Psychoanalytic Study of the Child* in 1951 and 1953, it was in 1954 that this major work was first published.

The words "child" and "children" appear in the titles of a good many of the writings of Martha Wolfenstein. This suggests her abiding interest in childrearing and child-training, not only in the United States but in France and England as well. One thing which distinguished Martha Wolfenstein from other clinicians and scholars concerned with children was her special expertise in children's fantasy behavior. The behavior she studied included how French children comported themselves in parks (1963b) or painted pictures (1963a) and how American children revealed their anxieties in riddling and joketelling, the subject of *Children's Humor*.

Wolfenstein was equally interested in fantasies by children, fantasies for children, and fantasies about children. This may be why she did not make the mistake of considering children as a separate entity apart from parents. In one of her studies of adult fantasies about children (1963c) contrasting selected Italian, French, British, and American films, she remarked, "Children as they appear in art, literature, drama, or films embody a complex mixture of fantasy and reality. They represent memories and dreams of adults about their own lost childhood, as well as feelings about those mysterious beings, their own children." The comparative outlook reflected in her film studies was also present in her brief but brilliant comparison of English and American versions of "Jack and the Beanstalk" (1963d). These essays, many of which can be found in Margaret Mead and Martha Wolfenstein, eds., *Childhood in Contemporary Cultures*, demonstrate not only her fascination with children and fantasy but also her important contributions to the difficult and often murky area of the study of national character.

In observing children, Martha Wolfenstein frequently focused on their reactions to various imposed stimuli. An early 1947 monograph was devoted to the responses of mothers and children to a children's story while one of her last studies (1965) tried to gauge the effect of the assassination of President John F. Kennedy upon children. In *Children's Humor*, this same experimental tendency may also be noted. Where the traditional anthropologist or folklorist might stop after having gathered his field data, Martha Wolfenstein fed selected portions of her data back to her informants. One of her goals was to differentiate the acquisition and perception of folklore on the basis of age.

She tested her hypotheses concerning age levels by intentionally introducing "advanced" riddles and jokes to children under six years of age to see if they could understand these materials. This combination of fieldwork and field experimentation is rare among anthropologists and folklorists.

The collection of jokes and riddles from children of different ages is a noteworthy achievement, especially since critical contextual data or personal biographical details about the informants are often provided. Yet it is Wolfenstein's ambitious attempt to correlate different forms of humor with different age levels that makes *Children's Humor* the pioneering work that it is. A recent comment (Sanches and Kirshenblatt-Gimblett 1976:71) calls the book "A classic study of the age factor in children's speech play" thereby echoing Erving Goffman's earlier praise (1955:284) for the "data presented on changes through age of the child's joking pattern." Strangely enough, the importance of this form of research appears not to have been fully appreciated until the early 1970s when rigorous follow-up studies began to be undertaken (cf. Weiner 1970, Shultz 1974, Prentice and Fathman 1975, Sutton-Smith 1976, and Zumwalt 1976).

Children's Humor is not diminished in value despite a number of criticisms that the sample of urban, mostly Jewish children from progressive private schools in New York City was not random enough, that Wolfenstein was evidently ignorant of previous collections of moron jokes and children's riddles by professional folklorists—she does not appear to be aware of the distinction between riddle and "catch,"—that Wolfenstein was strictly Freudian in her approach. A neglected classic, the book remains a landmark in the study of meaning in wit and humor. To this day, one can cite few comparable published instances of folklore fieldwork among children as young as five and six, which include not only texts in context, but an attempt to elucidate the possible underlying psychological significance of children's jokes and riddles.

Martha Wolfenstein's *Children's Humor* deserves to stand on the same bookshelf with Sigmund Freud's *Wit and Humor in the Unconscious* which inspired it and with Gershon Legman's encyclopedic two-volume series *Rationale of the Dirty Joke* and *No Laughing Matter* which followed it. Way ahead of its time in 1954 when it first appeared, *Children's Humor* is just as exciting and stimulating and insightful twenty-five years later. Many of the jokes and riddles reported by Wolfenstein are still actively transmitted among children as readers can easily attest by simply observing or questioning children around them. The scholarship devoted to the analysis of children's humor has remained scanty (cf. Borneman, Gaignebet, the Opies, and other references in Röhrich 1977:309-311), probably because it is not easy to make sense of nonsense, to find a rationale for the irrational. This is what makes Martha Wolfenstein's truly remarkable combination of fieldwork and analytic commentary all the more impressive.

ALAN DUNDES
University of
California, Berkeley

REFERENCES

Borneman, Ernest. 1973. *Unsere Kinder im Spiegel ihrer Lieder, Reime, Verse und Rätsel*. Studien zur Befreiung des Kindes, Band I. Olten und Freiburg.

———. 1974. *Die Umwelt des Kindes im Spiegel seiner 'verbotenen' Lieder, Reime, Verse und Rätsel*. Studien zur Befreiung des Kindes, Band II. Olten und Freiburg.

Freud, Sigmund. 1938. *The Basic Writings of Sigmund Freud*. New York.

Gaignebet, Claude. 1974. *Le Folklore obscene des enfants*. Paris.

Goffman, Erving. 1955. Review of *Children's Humor. American Journal of Sociology* 61:283-284.

Mead, Margaret, and Martha Wolfenstein. 1963. *Childhood in Contemporary Cultures.* Chicago. (First published in 1955.)

Opie, Iona, and Peter Opie. 1959. *The Lore and Language of Schoolchildren.* Oxford.

Prentice, Norman M., and Robert E. Fathman. 1975. Joking Riddles: A Developmental Index of Children's Humor. *Developmental Psychology* 11:210-216.

Röhrich, Lutz. 1977. *Der Witz: Figuren Formen Funktionen.* Stuttgart.

Sanches, Mary, and Barbara Kirshenblatt-Gimblett. 1976. Children's Traditional Speech Play and Child Language, in Barbara Kirshenblatt-Gimblett, ed., *Speech Play: Research and Resources for Studying Linguistic Creativity,* pp. 65-110. Philadelphia.

Shultz, T.R. 1974. Development of the Appreciation of Riddles. *Child Development* 45:100-105.

Sutton-Smith, Brian. 1976. A Developmental Structural Account of Riddles, in Barbara Kirshenblatt-Gimblett, ed., *Speech Play,* pp. 111-119. Philadelphia.

Weiner, Meryl. 1970. The Riddle Repertoire of a Massachusetts Elementary School. *Folklore Forum* 3:7-38.

Wolfenstein, Martha. 1947. *The Impact of a Children's Story on Mothers and Children.* Monographs of the Society for Research in Child Development, XI, no. 1. Washington, D.C.

———. 1951. A Phase in the Development of Children's Sense of Humor. *The Psychoanalytic Study of the Child* 6:336-352.

———. 1953. Children's Understanding of Jokes. *The Psychoanalytic Study of the Child* 8:162-173.

———. 1954. *Children's Humor:* A Psychological Analysis. Glencoe.

———. 1963a. French Children's Paintings, in Mead and Wolfenstein 1963, pp. 300-305.

———. 1963b. French Parents Take Their Children to the Park, in Mead and Wolfenstein 1963, pp. 99-117.

———. 1963c. The Image of the Child in Contemporary Films, in Mead and Wolfenstein 1963, pp. 277-293.

———. 1963d. Jack and the Beanstalk: An American Version, in Mead and Wolfenstein 1963, pp. 243-245.

Wolfenstein, Martha, and Gilbert Kliman. 1965. *Children and the Death of a President.* New York.

Wolfenstein, Martha, and Nathan Leites. 1950. *Movies: A Psychological Study.* Glencoe.

Zumwalt, Rosemary. 1976. Plain and Fancy: A Content Analysis of Children's Jokes Dealing with Adult Sexuality. *Western Folklore* 35:258-267.

Introduction

I

HUMOR is a distinctively human achievement: among living things only human beings laugh. Though jokes are fragile, transient, and generally slightly regarded productions, the ability to joke is an important emotional resource, and the psychological process involved in it an exceedingly complicated one. It would seem that we have mixed feelings about joking. While we tend to value highly the capacity for joking, and to disparage the humorless individual, every particular joke is apt to be quickly devalued, to lose its effect, to be forgotten. It is a truism that dramatic comedies quickly grow stale, while tragedies retain their impact across the span of centuries. Joking is a gallant attempt to ward off the oppressive difficulties of life, a bit of humble heroism, which for the moment that it succeeds provides elation, but only for the moment. The human situation still confronts us after this brief respite.

In joking we make light of disappointment and chagrin, transform painful feelings, and gain under the guise of foolishness some gratification for forbidden wishes.

These effects are achieved by means of complicated devices; as slight a thing as the joke appears, it is in its construction one of the most complex products of the human mind. The devices of joking are acquired in the course of a long process of development. It is the purpose of this book to trace some of the major aspects of this development from its beginnings in early childhood.

Being a child is a predicament fraught with special difficulties. Children are little and they greatly long to have the bigness and powers of the adults and their marvellous-seeming prerogatives; they feel often oppressed by adult superiority and coerced by adult moral rules. Children undergo much frustration and disappointment; they experience many anxieties which are hard for them to master. From an early age children avail themselves of joking to alleviate their difficulties. They transform the painful into the enjoyable, turn impossible wishes and the envied bigness and powers of adults into something ridiculous, expose adult pretensions, make light of failures, and parody their own frustrated strivings. We shall see particularly how young children (around the age of five) use joking to cope with their envy of adults, and how school age children turn their frustrated curiosity into a major theme of joking. While the particular exigencies which joking aims to alleviate vary with age, the basic motive of briefly triumphing over distress, of gaining a momentary release from frustration, persists. The adult never really attains the power which the child imagines he will have when he grows up. We are far from being masters of our world, and are lucky if we achieve a fraction of our desires. Thus humor remains a beneficent resource. Only complete omnipotence could dispense with it. The ancient Greek gods, who enjoyed only limited powers, made Olympus ring with their laughter. Only when divinity is conceived as omnipotent does laughter become superfluous to it.

The devices of joking vary with age. The requirements of what constitutes a satisfactory joke are different for children and adults, and subject to change through different stages of childhood. We shall see that the play on verbal ambiguity, a major technique of wit, has a long history. The requirement of brevity in wit becomes important only after a certain age. The amount of disguise which forbidden motives require for their joking expression increases with the progressive internalization of moral restraints, and occasions a series of increasingly complicated joke constructions. These are some of the technical aspects of jokes the development of which I shall attempt to trace.

In usual social discourse, to attempt to explain a joke spoils the effect. To enjoy a joke we must remain unaware of the devices by which it succeeds. On this ground it is sometimes felt that the analysis of the comic is a peculiarly humorless undertaking. But the analyst has a different aim from that of the comedian or wit, namely, to increase insight rather than to evoke amusement. Also what seems funny to children often seems quite unfunny to adults; that is in the nature of the present subject. Children's jokes are indeed apt to amuse adults mainly by their ineptitude, their inadequacy by adult standards, which may produce a comic effect, but different from the one the child gets. While the enjoyment of a joke involves an agreeable feeling of ease and effortlessness, the analysis of the very complicated structure of a joke has rather the opposite quality. I make these points so that the reader should not feel disappointed if he does not find this a funny book.

II

In interpreting jokes I have taken as basic the theory Freud developed in *Wit and Its Relation to the Unconscious*. Freud was led to study jokes when readers of his *Interpretation of Dreams* remarked that the dreams he analyzed (with their frequently surprising twists, puns, and so on) often sounded like jokes. He discovered that jokes resemble dreams in several ways. Though a joke makes more manifest sense than a dream (being a production of the waking mind and intended for communication), it also has a latent meaning which has undergone distortion and disguise. Freud found that jokes express sexual and hostile motives which would be condemned if they came out in more direct form. The semblance of foolishness (as the joke protagonist appears to be making some ridiculous error) or the verbal trick of wit distracts our attention from the underlying motives, which can thus be gratified without shame or guilt. In attempting to elucidate children's jokes I proceed on the assumption that they have a wealth of meaning, not all of which is evident on the surface. Some readers may be inclined to feel that I see more than is there, that these are simple and trivial forms of fun about which one need not inquire further. But when one hears one child after another repeat these same apparently trivial witticisms, and sees what value they attach to learning and telling them, one feels that there is a discrepancy between the intensity of their interest and the seeming triviality of the content. This gap can be filled in if we reconstruct the underlying meaning of the joke. It may be thought that the value of the joke is explained by its usefulness as a counter in the social game. While this is indeed an important function of the joke, it does not account for its specific form or content. There are many modes of social interplay; we must try to see what distinguishes the joking mode from others. Moreover, each joke has a particular content and our analysis will approximate completeness to the extent to which we can interpret each detail of this content.

In surveying the hundreds of jokes children told me, I have tried first to see what themes tended to recur. For instance, in the moron riddles so popular with children of six to ten, a recurrent motive for the moron's mad acts was that he had heard something or wanted to see something. This (taken together with other indications) suggested an underlying interest in investigation. To mention another instance, in many of the jokes told by children word play revolved around proper rather than common names (there were characters called Johnny Fuckerfaster or None-of-your-business). This directed my attention to the area of name play, of which I found simpler variants in younger children, and which gradually emerged as an important antecedent of word play.

In interpreting particular jokes or groups of jokes, I have utilized the following:

(a) Psychoanalytic findings about the meanings of various themes. While no particular symbol has an entirely uniform meaning, and individual, idiosyncratic connotations are always present or possible, there would seem to be nevertheless recurrent meanings which psychoanalysis has elucidated. So, for instance, if one interprets the comic effect of falling, one can draw on a range of typical emotional connotations of this act, any or all of which may contribute to its impact. There is the universal experience of learning to walk which makes falling in the literal sense a danger we have surpassed, while in fantasy falling retains a variety of associations of loss of control of impulses (as in a sexual fall, etc.) which underscore a

comic collapse with meanings in addition to, or counter-
pointed with, mere childish ineptitude. Thus in using psychoanalytic findings to interpret particular jokes or
comic themes, I have assumed that there are a number of
usual meanings which are apt to overdetermine the given
content, although any or all may not be present for a particular individual, while idiosyncratic meanings may be
operative in addition to, or in place of, the more common
ones.

(b) I have assumed the psychoanalytic scheme of emotional development as the framework against which to
plot the occurrence of different joke preferences at different ages. So, for instance, where I found a sharp change
in the style of joking from the age of five to six, a shift
from improvisation of original joking fantasies to the
learning and telling of ready-made jokes, I have related
this to the onset of what is called the latency period, the
period in which major emotional preoccupations of the
preceding phase undergo repression. Children at this time
become less free in spontaneous joking invention and seek
the safety and social sanction of the ready-made joke. I
did not start with a preconceived idea that there must be
a change in the style of joking with this change of phase,
much less of what this change would be; but I found a
marked discontinuity in the jokes and funny stories which
five- and six-year-old children told me, and then tried to
understand it in terms of the contemporaneous exigencies
of emotional development.

(c) As far as possible I observed the context in which
a joke was told or invented. This might be the immediate
situation in which a child produced a joke, where one
could see what he had just been thinking about; or it
might include facts about his present life situation or past
history. Thus where a six-year-old boy made a joke about

how absurd it would be to be able to write but not yet able to walk, it seemed relevant to know that he was on the one hand very ambitious intellectually, and on the other intensely envious of the advantage his baby sister had of being carried in his mother's arms.

(d) I have used children's associations to particular jokes or comic protagonists wherever I could obtain them. Children sometimes made spontaneous comments or explanations about their jokes, or elaborated on them in response to questions. So, for instance, with the joke about the fireman's red suspenders, some of them said it would be funny if he didn't wear suspenders and his pants fell down. This suggested that sexual exposure, while not manifestly expressed in the content of the joke, was an underlying theme. Other children talked about who wears suspenders and who doesn't, suggesting that another underlying theme was that of sex difference. Wherever possible I have used a combination of these means of interpretation.

These different grounds for interpretation evidently yield results of different degrees of probability. Where the joke is interpreted in terms of a child's associations to it or the immediate context in which it was told or produced, there is a relatively high degree of probability that the meanings I ascribe are present for the child, though not necessarily completely conscious. Where I connect up less immediate events of the child's life with a particular joke he invents or prefers, I become somewhat more speculative. The attempt to relate certain forms and themes of joking to a particular phase of development involves further assumptions; I am supposing that certain emotional experiences are relevant background factors without having established their presence in each case. When I infer that a frequent meaning of a certain theme as discovered in psychoanalytic observation attaches to that theme for other subjects in other circumstances, I am again on not too certain ground. It would have given my hypotheses a higher degree of probability if I could have checked them in each case by the children's direct associations. But children do not readily give associations (indeed it is assumed in child analysis that children cannot give free associations as adults do). So I often had to resort to round-about methods in reconstructing the meaning of children's jokes. If in the pages that follow I do not qualify each interpretation with a statement about its degree of probability (or constantly use such phrases as "it seems possible that" or "the hypothesis might be advanced," etc.), I hope the reader will understand that this is to avoid repetition and does not mean that I overestimate the degree of certainty of my statements. While the evidence for the interpretation of particular jokes varies from one instance to another, my aim has been to develop a coherent scheme in which various groups of jokes and various sequences in joke formation may be seen as interconnected. Thus the plausibility of the interpretation of any particular joke may, I hope, be enhanced by its coherence with the entire picture to be presented.

III

In the first chapter, on joking and anxiety, I discuss a basic motive of joking: the wish to transform a painful experience and to extract pleasure from it. Observing how children produce original jokes to help themselves out of distressing situations, I analyze the devices by which they achieve a transformation of feeling. I deal particularly with the predicament of children in relation to adults, their disappointment and envy in the oedipal phase, their longing to be big, and show how they express these themes in the funny stories they invent. These funny stories are the opposite of fairy tales; where in the fairy tale frustrated wishes are happily fulfilled, in the funny story such a fulfilment is presented as absurd or undesirable. The admired and envied size of the adults is exaggerated so that it becomes grotesque or incapacitating. The child's longing to have a baby, as the parents are able to do, gives rise to a story of a lady who has three hundred children, who all behave in an obnoxious way. Thus the pathos of the unobtainable is turned into comic improbability; the desirable is changed into its opposite.

In Chapter 2, on sex, names, and double meanings, I turn to a major formal aspect of verbal joking: play on the ambiguity of words. Word play, which for adults is a trivial and harmless kind of fun, has originally for children a more massive emotional impact. The effect of verbal ambiguity derives from two basic ambiguities: that of sex (am I male or female?) and that of emotion (am I loved or hated?). Early joking play on these ambiguities concentrates on proper names. Children of four make a joke of shifting the reference of proper names, playfully asserting that Mary is Johnny and vice versa. This may be traced to an earlier form of joke, observed in three-year-olds, calling a girl a boy, and a boy a girl. Playing on the meaning of what a person says is a sequel to shifts of sex and names. Since the young child is apt to feel wholly involved with his words, to feel that he is what he says, changing his meaning has a similar effect to changing his sex or his name. At first it is more disturbing than amusing. It is only as the degree of involvement with one's words becomes to some extent reduced that the transformation of their meaning can be taken as harmless and becomes a joke. Another line of derivation of word play proceeds from the double meaning of the proper name as a love name and a bad name. The child learns in his relation with his mother that his name can be used as an endearment or to underscore a scolding. A series of jokes of children from six to eleven express reactions to this ambivalent connotation of the child's name.

Chapter 3, on riddles and the legend of the moron, deals with a phase of development, the latency period, and the distinctive characteristics of the jokes which children in this period prefer. From the age of six to about eleven, children tend to identify jokes with riddles. They are at this time intensely preoccupied with the issue of smartness and dumbness, and their riddles serve in part the function of demonstrating that they are smart and the other fellow, who does not know the answer, is dumb. The joking riddle deals with knowing in a special way, by making a parody of questions and answers. In the preceding period of their lives, children have experienced strong sexual curiosity which has remained very incompletely satisfied. In latency, this earlier curiosity is to a considerable extent sublimated into more impersonal investigations, into the acquisition of school learning. The reaction to the previous disappointment and chagrin appears in the joking riddles, which constitute a comic accompaniment to the children's serious concern with learning. While in the riddles the subjects of earlier curiosity are pursued, this is done in a highly concealed way. The jokes present a harmless surface; their sexual import is almost entirely relegated to the latent level. The main protagonist in these jokes is the moron. He represents the child in his frustrated curiosity, impossible longings, and destructive rage, which become comic as the urgent impulses are translated into foolish mistakes. For latency period children, the moron is all they repudiate in themselves. They strenuously dissociate themselves from him, maintaining, for instance, that he could not be a child, but that he is a man of forty or fifty. The preferred jokes of latency period children, with their conciseness, verbal precision, and high degree of concealment, contrast with the original funny stories of five-year-olds. These younger children do not learn the joking riddles of their older playmates, but improvise rambling humorous fantasies of their own. The brevity and abrupt conclusion of the latency period jokes express an interference with this earlier free flow of fantasy. Thus the emotional needs of this age first give rise to what becomes a permanent formal aspect of joking: the brevity of wit. Another aspect of the preferred latency period jokes is that they require no artistry in the telling; it is only necessary to repeat the words correctly. This is markedly changed when children reach adolescence. For adolescents anecdotes replace riddles, and comic mimicry becomes a major component of joke telling. The joke teller impersonates the characters in the joke; he does not need to dissociate himself from them as drastically as latency period children do in the case of the moron.

Chapter 4 deals with the development of the joke façade. As inhibitions against the direct expression of sexual and hostile motives increase with age, increasingly complicated disguises are elaborated in the joking treatment of these themes. For a child of four or five it is a good dirty joke to shout at someone, "You're a doody!" or to relate, "A boy made pee-pee on the floor." With older children jokes on the same topic become progressively more complex. Word play and comic mistakes are introduced to mitigate the account of forbidden acts, and authority figures are blamed for them. There is also a disclaiming of responsibility, as the doing, the saying, and even the thinking of the forbidden are displaced from the joke teller to the characters in the joke. In aggressive joking the child first attacks the person directly before him. He then attempts to mitigate this by the pretense that it is not he who perpetrates the attack; he may maneuver his victim into assuming the responsibility for it. In a further development the attack is diverted to a third person at whom the joker and hearer can laugh together. Finally the attack is turned back against the self; the joke is at one's own expense.

In Chapter 5, I consider the development of children's understanding of jokes. Apart from the fact that children often do not understand particular jokes they hear (as shown by the incorrect ways in which they retell them), they have a more general difficulty in discriminating between joking and non-joking discourse. There are certain rules of joking distinct from those of reasonable talk, and children do not grasp this to begin with. So, for instance, they may give a serious answer to a joking riddle. As they get older they can reject such an answer as incompatible with joke conventions. Younger children sometimes protest that a joke is silly, that it does not make sense. Older ones recognize that not making sense in logical or realistic terms is definitive of the joke. There are certain stages in the development of this awareness, as gradually the two kinds of discourse, joking and non-joking, become differentiated.

In the Appendix, I indicate the data on which this study is based.

CHAPTER 1

Joking and Anxiety

I

AT A quarter past three there was only one child left in the kindergarten classroom, the others having been called for by mothers or maids or older brothers or sisters. The teacher came over to where the little boy sat quietly waiting and asked with some solicitude: "Who is calling for you today, Eugene? Your mother? Or Betty?" The boy smiled: "My mother is coming, and Betty is coming, and Kay is coming—the whole family is coming except me because I'm here already." He laughed.

In this joke the little boy transformed an anxious feeling into one of amusement. Let us see how this has come about. He takes the teacher's question as an occasion for reversing the situation, as if to say: It is only you and not I who is worried whether anyone is coming to call for me—and how ridiculous you are to doubt it. He is helped to this retort by a rather precocious tendency to turn what the teacher says into nonsense. Here he says something nonsensical himself (I am not coming because I am already here) in order to make nonsense of the teacher's concern.[1]

But to understand Eugene's little joke more fully we must know that his father has died in the past year. The thought "the whole family is coming" contains the wish: and my father too. This is immediately renounced with the word "except": the whole family is coming except one. But what would have been a direct expression of the sad reality is in its turn warded off with the substitution of himself for his father. Instead of "all except Daddy because he is dead," he produces "all except me because I'm here already." This gives the impression of being nonsense as he pretends to convey information while what he says is self-evident.[2] The little boy's substitution of himself for his father in the joke repeats what has happened in life: the father has died and the five-year-old boy has been left alone with the mother and two older sisters. The nonsense in the joke expresses the thought: But it is nonsense to suppose that I could take my father's place. As in the case of nonsense in dreams, it represents opposed wishes: I did and did not wish for my father's death. Thus the nonsense has a double application: the boy disposes of the doubt—which he imputes to the teacher—that anyone is coming for him; and, on a deeper level, he repudiates the wish to take his father's place. In yet another way this joke may have served to ward off anxiety. Waiting for his mother or sister the little boy may indeed have wondered whether they were ever coming, whether they might not also be dead. And this may have evoked fears of his own death. In saying, "I am here," he is affirming: I am alive.

The human capacity to transform suffering into an occasion for mirth is thus already at work in a five-year-old. Under the strain of separation from the mother and sisters with whom he expected to be reunited at this moment, and which evokes the tragic and permanent separa-

tion from the father, he is able to joke. He might instead
have been overwhelmed with anxiety; he might have cried
in the teacher's arms. Or he might have struggled to repress his painful feelings, to be apathetic. But he wants
to continue to feel, and he insists on feeling something
pleasant. He might then have forgotten his actual situation and become absorbed in play. He does not do this
either; he remains aware of his situation of lonely waiting.
While confronting this reality, he transforms his feeling
about it from pain to enjoyment. This retaining of contact with a disappointing reality combined with the
urgent demand to continue to feel, but to feel something
pleasant, is decisive for joking. However, the little boy
could not have achieved this transformation of emotion
if the teacher had not been there. She offers him sympathy which he refuses to accept, preferring to mock her.
Repudiating the teacher's pity, he is able to ward off self-
pity.

The wish to transform a painful situation in a joking
way frequently occurs without the production of a successful joke. We have then the sheer emotional readiness for
joking, what I would call the wish to joke. One struggles
against succumbing to a painful emotion and is resolved
to laugh instead, but no joke emerges. The emotional
shift, which is otherwise mediated by the joke, occurs by
itself. Or rather, more often, there is an effort to achieve
this emotional shift without quite succeeding. Alfred is a
ten-year-old boy who is greatly inclined to use joking as
a defense against unpleasantness. While he makes many
successful jokes, there are some occasions when he is only
able to express the wish to joke. For instance, he is reading with me the beginning of *The Count of Monte Cristo*
in which the death of the captain and his burial at sea are
described. He interrupts the reading to say: "This is a

funny story." "Why? Because the captain dies?" "Yes."
Alfred has fears about his father's dying. The death of
the captain in the story evokes anxious feelings about his
father which he would like to get rid of. But he is unable
to transform the painful material in any way; he can
only assert that it is funny. On another occasion he
is composing a picture story with marginal comments.
Where one of his characters is killed, he writes: "Dead.
Ha. Ha." Again he expresses the sheer wish to laugh so
as not to feel painful emotions. Alfred was studying with
me some school subjects which were difficult for him. He
was afraid that his having to work with me meant that he
was stupid or crazy. One day he found on a shelf my book
on the movies. When he read on the dust jacket that I had
made studies of the literary tastes of children and of the
insane, he produced prolonged hollow laughter.

How does the wish to joke develop into the production
of a joke? The transformation of one's own distress into
amusement does not always make a joke. Alfred may
assure us that the account of the captain's death is funny,
but, even if he succeeds in being amused, we are not
amused. Something in the content of the disturbing situation must be transformed to produce a joke. Then the
joker, in addition to changing his own feelings (and probably more successfully than by the mere wish to joke),
induces a similar emotional process in others. Let us observe how Alfred's wish to joke gives rise to a witticism.
He is writing a story in which an episode of violence and
death occasions some anxiety. Two crooks have robbed a
candy store and shot the proprietor. The proprietor's
body is laid in a bier. Alfred then improvises with considerable satisfaction: "a bier marked Rheingold." Here
the transformation of feelings for which he strives is reflected in the content of the joke. He has found a word

whose alternative meanings express on the one hand the total deprivation of the grave (bier) and on the other oral gratification (beer). Through the shift from one meaning to the other he provides the stimulus for us to participate in his emotional process. Moreover his own amusement is greater than when he simply tries to suppress painful feelings with his "ha, ha." He has the image of the pleasure-giving beer with which to ward off the ominous prospect of the bier. He has introduced a new image which corresponds to the pleasant feeling which he wants to have. The episode which Alfred has composed, the robbery of the candy store, expresses a violent and destructive grabbing of something pleasant to eat. The proprietor of the candy store represents the adults, the parents, who withhold such pleasures from the child and so arouse his violent impulses. The proprietor is accordingly killed. But this in turn arouses guilt. Alfred can mitigate this guilt by saying in effect: I do not mean to consign you the bier; rather I give you beer. Thus he makes a restitution for the oral pleasures which he has violently snatched. Such a mitigation of his own destructive impulses is also intended in his wish to joke on the other occasions which we have observed. When he maintains that the captain's death is funny, or writes "Dead. Ha. Ha." after his original fantasy of a murder, he is trying to say: It is all in fun; my murderous impulses are not serious. A denial of his dangerous impulses is combined with the wish to ward off anxiety about possible damage or death to himself.

In the "bier marked Rheingold" a shift from painful to pleasant feeling is expressed through a play on words. A word which connotes destruction is found to have another and quite opposite meaning. This is the reverse of those nineteenth century prints which bore the foreboding

message: In the midst of life is death. There one would
see a beautiful woman looking at herself in the mirror.
But looking again one would observe that the whole com-
position assumed the shape of a skull. The joke seems to
assert on the contrary: In the midst of death there is
bountiful life. Or rather, what makes it a joke is that it
asserts that they are the same. The discovery that the
same sound can mean a coffin and a pleasant drink has
for the unconscious the effect of a magical transformation. But this magical thinking is repudiated on the conscious level. Critically regarded it appears as an absurd
confusion, as if one had mistaken a "bier" for a "beer."
The imperious demand for pleasure even in the face of
catastrophe conceals itself in the guise of an error. The
joker pretends to be so foolish that, having found a
specious ground for equating the deprivational and gratifying, he mistakes the one for the other.[3]

A twelve-year-old boy draws a picture titled, "Custer's
Last Stand": it shows a man with a fruit stand. Here
again the horror of annihilation is transformed into, or
mistaken for, oral gratification. The boy wards off the
image of the piled up corpses and substitutes an appetiz-
ing heap of fruit. Custer who led his men into bloody
death becomes a kindly provider of food. In playing on
the word "stand," the boy pretends to have mistaken its
meaning. It is as if he said: Stand?—ah, you mean a
fruit stand. The wish to transform the grievous into the
gratifying finds expression in a pretended misunderstanding. It is true that for the unconscious oral gratification
and death may be equated, in the persistent infantile
fantasy of blissful merging with the mother's breast
which is also annihilation.[4] But on the conscious level this
thought is disparaged. The boy who makes the joking
picture knows very well that Custer's last stand was not

a fruit stand; he only pretends to confuse the two. The unconscious fusing of opposites, subjected to the light of conscious criticism, appears as an absurd mistake.

The joking transformation of feelings is not the same thing as a consolatory juxtaposition of the gratifying and painful. The exhortation to eat, drink and be merry for tomorrow we die is no joke. There is here no comic confusion of enjoyment and deprivation. The pleasurable is proposed as an anodyne to the painful, while the awareness of the imminent end of enjoyment contributes intensity, justification, and an admixture of sadness. In a painting by a French adolescent, we are shown a funeral cortege passing through a city street; in the foreground there is a restaurant and opposite a confiserie with many delicacies in the window.[5] While these evocations of oral pleasure mitigate the impact of the funeral, the effect is quite different from that of the "bier marked Rheingold" and of "Custer's Last Stand" (the fruit stand). The sad and the pleasurable are clearly distinguished. On ancient Roman sarcophagi there were sometimes reliefs of bacchanalian revels. This effort to transform a grief-stricken into a manic mood, or to give mystical affirmation to the unconscious fantasy of the union of death and life, is not comic either. The touch of reasonable mockery, which exposes the confusion of intoxication and death as an absurd mistake, is absent.

The obstacles which oppose the satisfaction of human wishes are manifold. Not only outer circumstances but inner constraints prove obstructive, constraints which are related to a fear of one's own impulses. Many wishes can obtain only an imaginary satisfaction, in a dream, a story, a joke. One of the specific nuances of the joke is the assurance that impulses are harmless. The joker does not intend to carry out any damaging action; he is only joking. Robert, another ten-year-old boy, is obsessed with destructive fantasies. He composes a story about a bad boy, Jack, in which various chapters are titled: "Jack wrecks the house," "Jack wrecks father," "Jack wrecks mother," "Jack wrecks everything," "Nothing stops Jack." Family life in this story is a series of quarrels frequently giving way to free-for-all fights. But the fighting has a slapstick quality: on the one hand the violence is abrupt and extreme, on the other hand no real damage is done. The combatants always emerge unscathed. Through his hero, Jack, who so brazenly wages war on his parents, Robert tries to reduce his disturbance about his own destructive impulses: it is all very funny. As he plans a new episode in which the chandelier will fall on father's head, or Jack will push mother through a hole in the floor, or will make a bomb to blow up the house, Robert's usually troubled face lights up and he laughs over it. As he writes, he repeatedly asks for my reassurance: "It is funny, isn't it?" He also insists that his parents read over what he has written and laugh about it. He wants the assurance that they do not condemn him for his destructive wishes. If they find the story funny it means that they regard his impulses as harmless. Since Robert's doubts on this point persist, he requires an amused response to his story over and over again. He reads it to his aunts, to his little brother, to his class in school. We can see in this one of the motives of the habitual joker, who requires ever renewed assurance that the impulses he expresses are innocuous. We can also understand the joker's distress when he fails to obtain an amused reaction. He then feels that his underlying bad wishes have been perceived and condemned.

Under the pressure of conflicting wishes children discover a joking way of dealing with them. The conflict may

be translated into a contradiction which they then regard
with a lofty reasonableness as if to say: But that's absurd! In this way they gain a momentary respite from
inner stress. Six-year-old John is an intellectually ambitious little boy, eager to learn to read and write. His
father discusses scientific subjects with him and John
strives anxiously and pridefully to master them. At the
same time he has intense longings in the opposite direction. When he sees his parents carry his baby sister in
their arms he is overwhelmed with the yearning to be carried in this way himself. However, when he pleads with his
parents to carry him, they protest that he is now too big.
At such moments he must wonder what is the good of his
intellectual attainments; growing up only debars him
from what he wants most. John makes up this riddle which
he considers funny: "Why did the moron write on a piece
of paper?—'Cause he couldn't walk yet." The combination of being able to write but not being able to walk, so
that one would have to be carried, represents the fulfilment of both of John's opposed wishes. In making a joke
of this impossible consummation, he stresses its paradoxical character: What an absurd idea to be able to write
and not to be able to walk yet! He uses his critical rea-
soning powers to devalue his frustrated wishes. We shall
see how often children, in their joking, attempt to free
themselves from impossible wishes by picturing their fulfilment as ridiculous.

II

The impossible longings of children, to whom so many
wonderful-seeming adult prerogatives are denied, give rise
to numerous fantasies, and provide the source for legends
and stories in which the frustrated wishes find their fulfilment. In such stories tiny heroes confront huge giants

and conquer them, obtain magical means for changing their size, or seven league boots by which they can overstep vast distances in a moment. The poor little girl can marry the great prince and kill the wicked witch who tries to stand in her way. Here the limitations of reality are set aside, and the wished-for becomes the rule of life. But the same wishes can also be dealt with in a joking way. Then the story is different. The wish fulfilment appears absurd, or impossible, or fraught with undesirable hazards. The same wishes that are gratified in a fairy tale are made the subject for mocking repudiation. In a fairy tale the hero may become small to escape attack, or big to overcome his enemies. In the humorous treatment of such transformations things turn out in a less gratifying way. Alice in Wonderland gets big when she wanted to get small and vice-versa. The fairy tale hero frequently obtains magical means for satisfying his wishes, a tablecloth which at a word is spread with a wonderful feast, a lamp which controls a supernatural servitor. The comic counterpart of this occurs when the prospect of wishfulfilment goes all askew, as in the story of the poor man and his wife who were granted three wishes. Absentmindedly the hungry man wishes he had a sausage. The sausage immediately appears. The wife, enraged at a wish having been wasted for such a trivial object, exclaims impulsively that she wishes the sausage was stuck to the end of her husband's nose. The third wish is then used up in detaching the sausage. When the prospect of wishfulfilment turns into frustration, it has a comic effect. While the fairy tale hero gains control over his world, the comic protagonist is repeatedly confronted with his inability to control things. The anxieties which attend the wishfulfilment fantasy are represented in the fairy tale by the obstacles and dangers which the hero or heroine must sur-

mount; in the joking fantasy they are utilized to make
the wishfulfilment seem not worthwhile. Thus joking becomes a means for the chastening of wishes, a device of
renunciation.

In many joking stories of children of five and six, who
are struggling to master their oedipal wishes, we can observe how wishfulfilment is turned into something ludicrous or grotesque.[6] A little girl's longing to marry her
father gives rise to a fantasy of an absurdly unsuitable
match. The envied capacity of the mother to have children
is expressed in a funny story of a woman with a hundred
children who all shout nonsense at once. The desirable is
presented in a frustrating way. Huge size becomes incapacitating. We find here the opposite of the mechanism
which we observed earlier by means of which the disturbing was changed into the gratifying (as in the transformation of "bier" into "beer"). The desired involves painful feelings because it is unobtainable, or because its at-
tainment would have fearful consequences. In the mocking of wishfulfilment, it receives an admixture of the dis-
agreeable in order to reduce its attraction. Perhaps when
the wished-for is treated in this comic way, anxiety about
the dangers of pursuing it has for the moment taken
precedence over its attractiveness.

A five-year-old little girl, Nora, turns an oedipal wishfulfilment fantasy into a funny story in this way. She
says that she will tell me "a very silly poem. It's a joke.
One day my grandfather went out walking. He met a
lamb. Haha. He said to the lamb, 'Will you marry me?'
Haha. And the lamb said, 'Baah,' because it didn't know
what to say. That's a funny one. A silly one." Here the
child has disguised the characters in her oedipal drama,
substituting her grandfather for her father and turning
herself into a little lamb. Such disguises occur frequently

in myths and fairy tales, where the closest, incestuous relations are transformed into relations between remote
creatures, as here a human being and an animal. The disguise serves to avoid the guilt and fear which would be
roused in acknowledging the true identity of the protagonists. The little girl who, while availing herself of this
disguise, finds it funny, has proceeded to take the fantasy
literally: How absurd it would be for grandfather to propose marriage to a little lamb. Thus having indulged in a
dream-like fantasy, she turns upon what she has produced
with a reasonable, realistic criticism. The comic effect is
achieved by a shift of level, from fantasy which uses a
symbolic mode of expression to literal-minded everyday
thinking. By this shift the fantasied wishfulfilment is
laughed off as ridiculous. The child has used a further
defense against her wishes; she has projected them onto
the father-figure in her little story. The grandfather is
the one who proposes the improper alliance to the little
lamb. The lamb remains demure and only emits a non-
commital "Baah." Thus the little girl suppresses her own
response to the tempting situation which she has conjured
up, blanking it out with a meaningless sound. But again,
taking it literally, she finds this dialogue comic: What
kind of answer is that to a proposal of marriage if one
can only say, "Baah?" It is in effect a mocking response.
The little girl, in the guise of the lamb, brushes off the
gratifying advances of the father. The comic treatment
of the wishfulfilment fantasy consists in repudiating the
gratification momentarily offered in imagination but in
fact unavailable. The pathos of the unobtainable is transformed into the absurdity of the improbable.

    The child, excluded from the parents' nocturnal inti-
macy, feels impelled, out of anger and envy, to interrupt
them. Nora turns this oedipal frustration also into a

funny story. As in her fantasy of grandfather and the little lamb, she represents herself as an animal. But this time the animal, excluded rather than courted, ceases to be demure and behaves in an obstreperous and uncontrolled way, which precipitates violent punishment. Here is her story, which was told with considerable excitement and mirth. "Once upon a time there was a little cat. And he meowed so much, he woke everyone up in the night." She laughs and jumps up and down. "And then," more jumping, "everyday he made on people's clothes. And then the tamer threw him out the window." She laughs. "Then he jumped back in the window. And the cat meowed and made in the box this day. And then the pussy cat meowed because he couldn't find his master. And then he wished that he had never done this again. Make a lot of O's" (on the page where I am writing this down) "cause that's his bowels. And then he made a crooked bowel. And then he began to have diarrhea. He made so much bowels he got diarrhea. It began to rain and he couldn't go out again. And then he wished he had never said raindrops should come again. He wished the raindrops would stay there for night after night. And then he was very sorry indeed. And he wished he had never done anything bad this week. I said it so crazy. And he was a very bad—punch, punch." She punches herself.

In this story the child (cat) disturbs the parents at night by crying, soiling and wetting. Young children frequently express nocturnal excitement by wetting or soiling, and they also attribute to these acts the power of breaking in on the parents' love-making.[7] The aggressive soiling of the cat dominates the situation in the household. Nora ascribes to the cat excretory liberties which she would not permit herself, and finds this continuous brazen naughtiness funny. It also achieves a wished-for

effect; the master, representing the father, is forced to
turn his attention to the cat and becomes very violent towards it, which is in part gratifying. But he wants to get
the disturbing little creature out of the way (throws it
out the window) and also withdraws from it (the cat cannot find its master). The cat's efforts to reform are un-
successful. The wayward defecating by which it at first
controls the situation ends by getting beyond its own control ("he made so much bowels he got diarrhea"). Similarly the rain which the cat produced by its wishes has
a boomerang effect in the penalties it involves. The cat
becomes "very sorry indeed." Nora concludes by acknowledging the naughtiness in the story as her own: she playfully punches herself. The story has a cautionary moral,
as the child implicitly recognizes that, if she would follow
her impulses to be naughty and disturb the parents, it is
she who would suffer.

Nora uses various devices to make her story funny. She
assumes a tone which expresses: This is all nonsense, not
to be taken seriously ("I said it so crazy"). The idea of
unrestricted soiling is funny for her. She enjoys for a
moment a vicarious release of impulse by means of a creature to which she attributes fewer inhibitions than she has
herself. (Adults often use the image of the child for similar comic effects.) While she cannot for long put aside the
thought of the penalties which such impulsive freedom
would evoke, she transforms the punishment itself into
comedy by making it abrupt and extreme. It would not
have been funny if the master had simply scolded or hit
the cat; it is the extreme gesture of throwing it out the
window which makes it comic. Children frequently find
such sudden and extreme violence funny. As the misbehaving cat is immediately precipitated out of the window,
there is no gradual building up of apprehension, no time

to develop a reaction of distress. The extremity of the act also tends to make it unreal: this couldn't happen. By exaggeration, the violent or dangerous is transformed into the comically improbable. There is also a subtler comic effect in the way in which everything gets out of control for the naughty cat. Using its excretory powers to get its own way, it is then overwhelmed by the forces it has released, and obtains the opposite of the wished-for results. The inept comic protagonist is, as we noted, the opposite of the fairy tale hero with his successful magic.

Thus we see how a five-year-old little girl uses joking as a means of mastering her oedipal wishes. She imagines oedipal gratification in the ridiculous guise of grandfather proposing to a little lamb; and she turns her protest against oedipal frustration into a story of comical mishaps of a naughty cat.

III

The small size of children in comparison with adults, and the long long time it will take for them to grow up, lead to compensatory fantasies of being at once very big. These fantasies about size and the distress about being small may be treated in a comic way by exaggeration. The small may be made so minute that ambitions and expectations in connection with it cannot plausibly be maintained. Paradoxically exaggeration of the large can also reduce its impact. The presumed claims of the large are expanded to a point where they cease to be credible. Reasonable criticism is turned against the exorbitance of fantasy to make it appear funny. Comic effects are also achieved through reversals, in fantasies of huge babies like Rabelais' Gargantua, and conversely in reducing the great to diminutive proportions, as in the case of the rulers of Lilliput. Children frequently imagine that as they

grow big their parents will grow small.[8] Picturing such a
result literally may have a comic effect. The hero of Al
Capp's comic strip, Li'l Abner, is a huge though childish
figure, while his parents, whom he refers to as "my li'l old
pappy" and "my li'l old mammy" are half his size.

Contrasts of large and small have a multiplicity of references. Besides the comparison of the total body size of
the child and the adult, there is the difference between the
little boy's penis and the father's, and there is also the
discrepancy between the girl's clitoris and the male genital.[9] Children take the clitoris to be a tiny penis and
imagine it may grow. Fantasies of changing size may also
refer to the potentialities of the penis for getting larger
and smaller. The changes in size which Lewis Carroll's
Alice undergoes express a combination of these themes:
the child's feeling of being very small in comparison with
the grown-ups and wish to reverse this relation, the fantasy that the girl's tiny organ will grow, and the transformations of the girl-as-phallus, showing such surprising and alarming capacity for erection.[10]

Five-year-old Ann develops a fantasy intended to be
funny, in which a girl appears alternately as very little
and very big. She is concerned with her own smallness and
wish to be big, and also with the smallness of her genital,
her lack of a male organ. At one moment she tries to console herself for this smallness or lack by comically exaggerating it to the point of incredibility; at the next she
indulges in fantasies of grandiose size which she also carries to a ludicrous extreme. She first gives this version:
"Once upon a time there was a little girl as little as a
mouse. Her hair was as long as that box. She didn't have
any eyes or any mouth or any nose or any stomach or any
legs. She didn't have anything. Nothing. She was just
nothing." [11] Here after giving the little girl one dispro-

portionately large body part ("hair as long as that box" —the box being the size of a packing case), Ann presents an unbelievable list of missing parts. As she knows that she in fact does not lack the parts she mentions, this has a consoling effect. In a second version of this story, she introduces more elements of exorbitant size, which, however, continue to alternate with extreme minuteness. It is as if she cannot decide which device is more satisfactory for making light of her discontent about size. Here is the second version: "Once upon a time there was a little tiny girl as big as a mouse. Her hair was as big as the whole world. And her arms were as big as the moon. Her feet were bigger than anything." Some other little girls who were listening interpolated that the stars are even bigger than the sun. Ann incorporated this point: "I mean her feet were as big as stars. She really was tinier than a mouse. She had to live in a bead because she was much tinier than a mouse. Tinier than a germ. When she went into the garden, the garden was much tinier than she was." Ann's fantasies about a girl of paradoxical proportions have a further determinant besides her concern with the size of her own body and body parts. Ann is plagued by a little sister. The tiny girl who nevertheless takes up such an excessive amount of space (in the household, in the mother's affections) is thus also the baby sister. In her effort to laugh away her annoyance with the baby, Ann says in effect: How can anything so little be so big (important)?

The imposing and frightening size of the father's genital may also be made comic by exaggeration. A six-year-old girl, Rita, draws a picture of a man with hugely extended ears, topped by a hat of even more disproportionate size. She then relates: "Once there was a funny man. He had ears on one side and ears on the other. His hat

was as big as the world." She laughs. "When people tried
to walk they couldn't. Every time they had to jump inside
his hat." She thus makes a joke of the size of the penis,
which she symbolizes as a hat, and of its procreative power
(all the people inside it). She exaggerates the size of what
the man has so that it becomes first incongruous (the
oversized ears and hat), then incredible (as big as the
world). She also jokingly reverses the procreative process
by which, according to her fantasy, the paternal phallus
has created everyone; having emanated from this source,
everyone must now jump back in. While this may represent a wishfulfilment fantasy of loving reunion, it is subjected to mocking criticism as she recognizes that it is
impossible. The desired consummation is also presented as
most inconvenient. The paternal phallus expanding to re-
encompass all its progeny interferes with the capactiy for
independent movement which they have achieved: "When
people tried to walk they couldn't. Every time they had
to jump inside his hat." Striving to outgrow her childish
wishes, she depicts their fulfilment as entailing more loss
than gain.

Another joking fantasy of exaggerated size plays with
the image of the pregnant mother. Five-year-old Ann,
having listened to the story of the man whose hat was as
big as the world, was inspired to compose a story about
an old lady whose house was as big as the world. The same
consequence follows that no one can get out of this house.
The bigness of the house (house being a frequent symbol
of the female body) becomes a nuisance not only to others
but to the lady herself, who is unable to get out of the
house. Ann mocks the pregnant mother by stressing her
incapacitation, in part projecting onto the mother her
own frustration and distress. She transforms an enviable
situation into one of comic annoyance. The wished-for is

laughed off by playing up and exaggerating its inconvenient aspects. Here is Ann's story: "Once there was an old lady who lived in a house. A great big house as big as the world. That's why everybody had to walk straight in her house. Every time they tried to walk out of her house they couldn't. Because their house was in her house too. Every time they tried to play a game they had to play in her house of course. Every time they tried to move their bed out of her house they couldn't. This old lady did not like that. Every time she got cross every person she got cross at would try to get out, to get out the window. They couldn't. The window was too small. And when she went shopping she had to go shopping at her house. And when she ate, she couldn't eat at a restaurant. The restaurants were all in her house. Now this old lady got too tired of this one day. And she said to someone: 'Why do I have to do all these things in my house?' And one day she got much too tired and she said: 'I guess I'll get out of this house.' But she went over to the door and it was locked. It was no use. And besides she wanted to get out but she couldn't. Finally she saw someone coming in the door. 'Well, that door wasn't locked. I wasn't pushing.' Just then she saw water splashing over the house. 'Oh dear! what shall I do? Water is splashing into my house. What shall I do? Oh, oh, oh!' Then she called the water man. The water man said: 'You want all this water taken out of your house?' And the water man said: 'I'll have to get my tools to do this. It's just too much for me.' Then the water man said: 'I did this already.' Then the water man went away." The story was interrupted at this point; in a continuation of it a few days later, the old lady was still left in the same predicament.

Here the little girl, who has envied her mother's recent pregnancy and cherished the impossible wish to be preg-

nant herself, transforms the wished-for into a nuisance.
The mother's body (house) is so big that she cannot go
anywhere. There is also the question so puzzling to children: how does the baby get out? (We shall see that this
is the theme of a series of joking riddles of children over
six, about the predicament of a man in a locked house.)
In Ann's story, the pregnant mother, confined to the
house, is condensed with the baby in the womb: neither the
mother nor the other people (babies) can get out. There
is also probably her own wish to escape from the mother
(to get out of the house) which she is unable to realize.
The water man is the father, who, according to the child's
fantasy, makes water in the mother. The enviable position
of the mother in this respect also is transformed into the
opposite and becomes only troublesome for her. Her huge
house, her consequent confinement, her being inundated
by the water man are all sources of annoyance. Thus the
little girl tries to mitigate her frustration and envy by
presenting the wished-for as beset with comic catastrophes.

Another starting point for fantasies about size discrepancies is the relation between the vagina and penis. The
female genital may be imagined as too small so that the
male will get stuck in it; or the female may be imagined
as too large so that the male becomes engulfed. As with all
the other questions of size, this is a source of anxiety, but
it may also be turned into something funny. A five-year-
old boy draws a picture of a funny man with huge feet.
He then relates: "A big pig in a little house, and he gets
all smashed. He doesn't like it. And he has a small window
with a big head going through it. And he jumps his head
right back in." Thus he starts with an image of the great
size of the male genital (the disproportionately large
feet of the funny man). This is then opposed to the disproportionately small female genital (the little house in

which the big pig gets smashed). He proceeds to reassure himself, again changing the image, that a big head can go in and out of a small window. Another five-year-old boy produces a funny story in which the size discrepancy is in the opposite direction: the female genital appears as a huge red field in which the male is completely buried. "Once there was a red field. A farmer went in. And you know where the seeds were? In his mouth. And he couldn't plant because there were no seeds. You know why? Because he ate all the seeds up. So he dug a hole and buried himself. And he grew to be a carrot and a tomato and a potato." The farmer having swallowed the seeds probably expresses fantasies of fellatio and oral impregnation. But the farmer with the seeds inside is also the penis, which must be buried in the red field so that the seeds may be planted. This expresses the fantasy that the father's penis is incorporated by the mother. However, in the reassuring conclusion a carrot (penis) and a tomato and potato (testicles, which had apparently also been incorporated) reemerge. The means by which this becomes funny is, as in previous instances which we have analyzed, by taking the symbolic representation literally, so that the farmer who has foolishly swallowed the seeds still more foolishly decides to plant himself. This anticipates some of the comically miscalculated and often self-destructive acts of the moron, the favored hero of the jokes of children over six.

The envied procreative powers of the parents may be made fun of by exaggeration, for instance, in fantasies of a family with hundreds of children. Just as the great size of the father's phallus or of the body of the pregnant mother were made ridiculous by being blown up beyond belief, so the baby which the child hopelessly longs to produce becomes less desirable by being multiplied a hundredfold. Also the power of the parents here passes into

loss of control: They cannot stop making babies. A six-
year-old girl tells the following: "Once there was a little
girl. A lady. And she had three hundred children in one
year. And they all went to school and they all had the
same group and they were all the same age. They all did
the same things at school. Wasn't that sil-lee? They all
had dirty faces. They all had pimples on their lips. And
they all had the same age. They all had dresses on. Some
were boys but they had dresses on too, hee, hee, hee. . . .
Then they all said the same thing at the same time. And
they all sang. The only song they knew was: Abbadabbadabba. . . . Their names were Jimmy and Mary and
Cocky" (she laughs) "and Ellen and Frances and Jona-
than . . . and Timmy and Bimmy and Kisser. The End."

One baby is an object of longing, but at the prospect
of three hundred babies all singing "Abbadabbadabba"
in unison motherly sentiment is dissipated. Thus a transformation of feeling is achieved by the multiplication of
its objects. The little girl uses additional devices to devalue the babies: they are dirty and diseased (they have
pimples on their lips), the boys are castrated (wearing
dresses), and they have silly or naughty names (Cocky,
Kisser). Another motive behind such a fantasy is the
child's anxious concern with how many more children the
mother may have. The motive of rivalry with possible
brothers and sisters complicates the wish to compete with
the mother. In producing the fantasy that the mother will
have three hundred children in one year, which she knows
is impossible, the little girl reassures herself: nothing is
going to happen.

The transformation of feeling by the multiplication of
its objects has a variety of comic applications. When a
stimulus is increased beyond a certain point the feeling
evoked is apt to diminish. This is so for the grievous as

well as for the desirable. Thus, for instance, Sacha Guitry
in *The Story of a Cheat* extracted comedy from the si-
multaneous death of twelve members of a family of thirteen. He expresses the feelings of a young boy who is the
sole survivor in this way: 'If one had died, I would have
mourned. Two or three would have been a catastrophe.
But twelve! Which should I mourn first? Which next? I
don't know. It's just impossible.' The boy following the
procession of twelve coffins shrugs his shoulders and looks
bewildered (as the sound-track conveys Guitry's reflections) and the impact on the audience is a comic one.
With a similar effect the hero in the British film, *Kind
Hearts and Coronets,* murders not one but half a dozen
relatives who stand between him and an inheritance. It
would seem that as the number of murders mounts, the
empathic guilt on the part of the audience declines. Of
course, there are numerous additional comic aspects in the
method of committing the several crimes which contribute
to the effect. The multiplication of instances does not necessarily in itself seem funny, but it reduces the emotional impact and thus facilitates the transformation into
comedy.

IV

We have seen how children find ways of making fun of
the bigness, power, and prerogatives of the grown-ups
whom they envy. There is another imposing aspect of
adults, which is often oppressive and fearful to children,
namely their moral authority; and here too children seek
relief through mockery. They seize with delight on opportunities to show that the grown-ups are not infallibly
good, or to expose the grown-ups' demands as absurdly
impossible, or to distort the meaning of a prohibition into
a permission. A little girl of five was very fond of using

words for more or less taboo body parts, such as "bottom." If her mother happened to say, "I think I put this or that in the bottom drawer," the child would shout delightedly: "You said 'bottom'!" Thus she pretended to catch her mother in the same naughtiness to which she herself was prone. In a joking way she attempted to make out that her mother was not so very good, and so to relieve herself from the pressure of a too ideal model.

In rebellion against adults' demands, children may try to reduce these demands to absurdity. A six-year-old girl tells me that her teacher said something funny. "She said we couldn't get up from our chairs until we'd finished eating. It sounded as if we'd have to sleep there all night!" In her wish to demonstrate that adults' demands are excessive, the little girl retorts mockingly in her own mind to what the teacher has said: And suppose we don't finish? Then you mean we'll have to stay here all night? By distorting the teacher's demand into something so unreasonable as to be ridiculous, the child exempts herself from feeling bound by it.

Children become skillful in misinterpreting what adults say, to find sanctions for naughtiness or exemption from chores. A teacher says to a four-year-old little girl: "Are you going to help me to put down the beds?" The little girl replies playfully, pretending to have misheard: "Yes, I'm going to help you to take off your head." Thus she pretends that the teacher has requested an all-out expression of the child's aggressive impulses, and she, being a nice little girl, will gladly comply. In the classroom of the six-year-olds, the teacher is teaching the children how to tell time. She has a large clock, the hands of which she places in various positions as she asks the children what time it is. As she puts the clock hands to three o'clock, she asks again: "What time is it now?" The children shout: "Three o'clock! Goodbye, teacher!" In an uproar of laughter they rush to put on their hats and coats and are half-way out the door before the teacher can stop them. Thus they pretend not to have understood the hypothetical character of the teacher's question, and to believe that she is pointing out the actual time to them, three o'clock, the end of the school day. They distort the teacher's meaning in such a way that it becomes an exemption from further work; it is she who sets the clock hands forward and lets them out of school. The embodiment of restrictions is transformed by their joking pretense into an agent of release.

Exposure of moral authorities and mocking compliance with their demands provide a theme for extensive comic elaboration. We shall later examine more complicated jokes in which older children express these motives. The struggle over morality, the difficult acceptance of its claims, the rebellious striving to free impulses from its restrictions, is a pervasive human predicament. The parents, the first embodiments of moral rules, present a dual aspect. On the one hand, they appear ideally good so that there seems to be no legitimate appeal from their righteousness even when it is hard and punishing; one must bow before it. On the other hand, there are moments when the parents appear fallible, weak, unreliable, indulging themselves in the very pleasures which they would deny their children. They appear capricious, dealing rewards and punishments according to whim rather than justice. At such moments the child feels that there is no moral order; what comes to him of good or ill is a matter of luck rather than an inevitable consequence of his goodness or badness.

The dual image of the parents, as righteous or fallible, provides the model for two opposing views of the world, the tragic and the comic. In tragedy the moral order is in the ascendant; the world is ruled by a righteous authority. The criminal brings down on his head all the punishment which such authority affirms to be his due. But in comedy the world appears under the sway of capricious and unreliable authorities. Their rewards and punishments are dispersed in an accidental rather than inevitable way, and they can often be deceived or circumvented. Correspondingly the comic hero neither deserves the hardships he undergoes—he is a harmless fool—nor does he, with his weaknesses, deserve what good fortune befalls him. This accidental character of the comic hero's fate may be observed in American film comedies. The hero, having triumphed as a result of chance circumstances, is by a further accident laid low at the last moment. In *The Kid from Brooklyn*, the hero, a complete weakling, wins a boxing championship because his opponent has been accidentally given a sedative and kicked in the head by a horse just before the match. At the end the hero is being congratulated by a crowd of admirers when an enthusiastic old lady, reenacting the fight, accidentally knocks him out.

The relation of the comic world to inadequate moral authorities is particularly evident when these authorities appear as characters in the drama. In Charlie Chaplin's *City Lights*, the little tramp encounters by chance an eccentric millionaire who befriends him. The millionaire's benevolence is, however, unpredictable. When he is drunk, he is extravagantly friendly to the little tramp, embracing him, feeding and clothing him, giving him an expensive car. But when he is sober, he fails to recognize the little fellow, has him thrown out of the house and abandons him to the police. Thus for the bewildered little tramp the world is presided over by a capricious deity.

The figure of the drunken millionaire is a composite of the fallible and bitterly disappointing parents of Chaplin's own childhood: his father who died of alcoholism when Chaplin was five and his mother who shortly afterwards went mad and failed to recognize her children.[12] Chaplin has turned this real life tragedy into dramatic comedy by extending the capriciousness of the parents into the rule that governs all events in his comic world. For the inescapable tie between father and son he substitutes the chance encounter of the little tramp with the millionaire. The father's death inevitably dragged the child down into misery. In the film, where the little tramp tries to save the millionaire from suicide, the latter almost drowns the little fellow through sheer drunken ineptitude. Thus a series of comic accidents is substituted for the inexorable links of real life relations. The sequence of events in the comic world, its hazards and its windfalls, are as unpredictable and capricious as the behavior of the parents.

How decisive the image of parental authority is for comedy or tragedy may be seen in the alternative interpretations of the *Merchant of Venice*. The comic or tragic effect depends on how the character of Shylock is regarded. Shylock is a father-figure who has been wronged and who claims vengeance. The issue is whether his claim is a righteous one. The comic impact, which the play originally had, depended on taking Shylock as an unworthy and ludicrous character; his pretense to justice could be unmasked as low vindictiveness. To the extent to which more recent interpretations of the play have tended to attribute justice to Shylock's position, and to see him as cheated of his due, he becomes invested with the paternal right to punish and the play loses its comic effect.

The little jokingly rebellious sallies in which children

try to expose the fallibility of adult authorities contain the principle which can later be extended into the comic view of life. We have seen how children in their disadvantageous relation to adults—being little, deprived of longed-for prerogatives, and subjected to moral restraints —can avail themselves of joking for relief. They can make the wished-for but impossible seem absurd; they can exaggerate the size and power of the grown-ups till it becomes ridiculous; and they can turn adult righteousness inside out. In these ways children strive to master their envy and their guilt towards the adults. But there is another aspect of the relation between adult and child which can be utilized for comic effect: that is when one regards oneself from the point of view of an indulgent and comforting parent and laughs at one's troubles as a small matter, not to be taken seriously. This is what Freud considered the essence of humor, as if one said to oneself: "Look here! This is all that this seemingly dangerous world amounts to. Child's play—the very thing to jest about!" [13] One might think that this kind of humorous consolation is only available to adults. The child is still a child; how can it comfort him to regard his present troubles as childish? However, what is childish is a relative matter. Children are in a continual process of outgrowing things and are inclined to look down as from a great distance on phases only recently surpassed. The child of three or so, who can walk securely, laughs uproariously at the faltering steps, the teeterings and topplings of a slightly younger one.

A child may jokingly console himself for present difficulties by assimilating them to more childish ones which no longer trouble him. Alfred, the ten-year-old boy of whom I have spoken before, uses this device to transform distress into a joke. Alfred felt humiliated that he had to work with me because of learning difficulties and was worried that I might consider him defective. One day he came in with his jacket and cap on backwards and remarked nonchalantly: "Some people think I'm backward. Isn't that ridiculous?" By shifting the meaning of "backward" he makes nonsense of the supposed criticism of the adult. It is as if he said: What do you mean "backward?" That I wear my clothes backward? That's ridiculous. He also makes a comic pretense of not noticing his patent backwardness (in the second sense). At the same time he is demonstrating that if he is backward it is because he purposely makes himself that way. (Alfred frequently tried to mitigate his distress over mistakes by making out that they were intentional.) But through the double meaning of "backward" he has also discovered a way of transforming his present difficulty into a more childish one which need not be taken seriously. Very young children who are just learning to dress themselves frequently put their clothes on backwards or inside out, and their mothers are apt to point out laughingly what they have done and set it right. Alfred invokes this earlier stage, whose difficulties now seem so harmless and trivial, in an effort to see his present problems in a similar light.

V

In the predicament of the child, who longs for so many things he cannot have, fantasy and make-believe play are major modes of satisfaction. In his fantasy and in his play the child can be the triumphant hero, replete with the powers and prerogatives which he otherwise lacks. He can be a king, a cowboy, a space-cadet; he has all sorts of weapons and equipment with which he can magically protect himself and work his will on others. He gladly loses himself in this gratifying world of fantasy and play, and though he remains aware that it is not real, a willing suspension of disbelief is in the ascendant. Joking is opposite to such play and fantasy. Instead of conjuring up the illusion of an unattainable situation, joking moderates the impossible wish. Instead of the child's imagining himself as big and strong, the image of bigness and strength is exaggerated to absurdity, or the child transforms his ineptitude into clowning. In all make-believe, joking or serious, in children's play and in fiction and drama, there is a dual attitude: we pretend that something is real and we know that it is not. But in serious make-believe the emphasis is on the illusion; at the comic end of the scale the stress is on its not being so. Events in serious fiction bear the same emotional sign that they would in reality; the difficulties of the hero involve our distress. But in comedy we are more aware that the embroilments of the comic hero are unreal, and the ineptitude or inappropriateness of his reactions facilitate our laughing at him rather than suffering on his behalf. Where serious make-believe works to alter reality in wished-for directions, joking changes rather our feelings about unwished-for events.

In a joking mood, a child may admit his inadequacies while making light of them; but resorting to make-believe play he grandly overrides his weaknesses. We have seen how Alfred could make a joke of his "backwardness," admitting it in a sense, but reducing it to something childish and slight that one need not take seriously. Thus he transformed a troubled feeling into one of amusement. In his make-believe play we can observe him following a different line. One day he asked me in a slightly self-mocking grandiose way whether I had sent off to the publisher the story he had written during the previous lesson. He thought he would ask thousands of dollars for it, but then, vacillating about the value of his work, asked me whether it was not worth only two cents. I told him quite seriously that I did not know whether his story could be published but that it was good work for a ten-year-old boy. He reacted to this with an exaggerated show of insulted indignation, and proceeded to initiate the following game. He was a publisher and I was his secretary. He had me read to him all the stories he had written and frequently interrupted with expressions of appreciation, proclaimed this Alfred X to be a great writer, and resolved to publish his work and pay him royally for it. Thus in play he rectified a humiliating situation. He demoted me from the position of authority, assumed this role himself, and so bestowed on himself the credit and worthiness of reward which I had withheld. His feelings of hypersensitive vanity remained unmodified, but he conjured up a situation in which they would be gratified rather than thwarted. His joking treatment of his doubts about his abilities took an alternative course. The frightening thought "Some people think I'm backward" could be uttered, but in such a way that the feeling about it was transformed. Instead of transporting himself to unreal greatness, he remained in the role of a little boy. Insofar as there was a distortion of reality (and the degree of the distortion seems less than in the make-believe play) it was in the opposite direction. By pretending to be a more infantile child he made his mistakes seem harmless and forgivable and at the same time enjoyed a momentary release from the pressure of his ambitions.

Eugene, the five-year-old little boy of whom I spoke at the beginning of this chapter, whose father had recently died, found different solutions to his emotional problems in jokes and in make-believe play. The little boy who had wished to take the father's place had undergone the tragic fate of having this wish granted. He then became haunted by the image of the father as a terrible avenger or as awesomely withdrawn in death. In his make-believe play he assumed the role of the frightening father; he did not have to be afraid but rather frightened the other children. Or he could be the strangely immobilized father; and again it would be another child who would wait in vain for signs of life from him. Thus in his play he transformed himself in an impressive manner; he ceased to be the sad or frightened little boy and became the strange or overpowering father of his fantasies. In his joking he remained the little boy, but he tried to see his situation as divested of danger. Everything became reduced to small and harmless dimensions. His own impulses were harmless; the grown-ups were silly people from whom one had nothing to fear; it was obvious that he was safely alive and would remain so.

Eugene's favorite game was to pretend that he was "a lion, a daddy lion that hasn't been tamed yet." He would pursue the other children with outstretched claw-like hands, frighten them and even attack and hurt them. Some little girls, fleeing from him, pleaded: "Be friendly to us, Eugene. You frighten us too much." The feeling of terror, which haunted his fantasies of his father, continued to pervade the play, but he succeeded in making the other children rather than himself suffer it. In another game, Eugene climbed into a large box and allowed his friend, Billy, to cover the top with boards so that only a small crack remained open. Billy explained that Eugene was a horse in a stall, and asked me to let him know if the horse neighed. But Eugene crouched grinning and motionless in a corner of the box and did not make a sound. I had the impression that the boy inclosed in the box represented the father in his coffin. By remaining silent while his little friend waited for a sound from him, he seemed to express: It is not I who wait in vain for a sign of life from the grave, it is he.

In Eugene's joke "The whole family is coming, except me, because I'm here already," he affirmed: I am here—alive. In the underlying thoughts of this joke as we reconstructed them, he seemed to repudiate as nonsense the idea that he could take his father's place. Thus while in play he assumes the father's role, in joking he makes light of the possibility of doing so. On another occasion he made a joke of a playmate's threat to attack him, at the same time demonstrating his own harmless and peaceable disposition. Following a quarrel Eugene and another boy were calling threatening taunts at each other. "I'll kick you." "I'll kick you back." After numerous repetitions of this, Eugene suddenly shifted to "I won't kick you back." The other boy, who was slow on the uptake, continued with "I'll kick you." Eugene replied grinning and shaking his head: "But I won't kick you back." Finally the other got it and laughed and Eugene laughed too. Here Eugene had apparently grasped the fact that no real kicks were being exchanged so that he could defeat the other boy more effectively by refusing to give the expected response than by giving the imaginary kick. He was demonstrating that he could not be controlled by the other and also that he had overcome the repetitious aggressiveness in himself. With joking pleasure he affirmed that he was not angry or dangerous and had nothing to fear from the imaginary attacks of the other. Thus in his joking Eugene is the opposite of the dangerous daddy lion of his play.

Eugene showed a precocious tendency to mock adults. By demonstrating how silly they were he reduced their impressiveness; the huge beings of his frightening fantasies for the moment dwindled away. With his teacher he used the technique of taking her words more literally than they were intended and so making out that she had said something foolish. When the teacher told another boy to put on his shoes, Eugene remarked: "He doesn't have shoes, he has sneakers." The teacher corrected herself: "I meant, 'Put on your sneakers.' " To this Eugene retorted: "I already have my sneakers on." By thus reducing an authority figure to absurdity Eugene seemed to be reassuring himself that the adults were harmless and that he had nothing to fear from them.

Children are not always serious in their make-believe play: they sometimes give it a joking quality. In serious play they evoke the illusion that they are the characters they impersonate. The characters, corresponding to admired adult roles, are represented in an ideal light, which the children consider correct; that is the way such personages should behave. The little boy with two guns playing cowboy is brave and dauntless; the little girl mothering her dolls is kind and good. But in joking play the children expose negative aspects of their models or endow them with incongruous traits. This is apt to be done in an exaggerated way, and the children feel that the characterization is not correct. The illusion of reality is reduced, the real and the ideal being closely related here. The child feels that the character he portrays is distorted, and he is less identified with the role, which has become a less desirable one. The little boy makes a joke of playing a cowardly cowboy; that is not a real cowboy, and he is more aware of just pretending than when he is a brave cowboy. Similarly the little girl may make a comedy of being an exaggeratedly cruel mother who beats and starves her children. A group of five-year-old girls were fond of playing school. While the child playing the teacher behaved in a decorous, efficient way, the game proceeded in all seriousness. But when one child, assuming the role of an exaggeratedly severe teacher, shouted at every turn: "I cannot allow that!" this evoked continuous laughter. The impersonation was a parody of the forbidding adult, and the incongruity between the little girl and her assumed authority predominated over the illusion of her acting. The momentary fright which may have been roused in the other children by the shouted reprimand was immediately dissipated in the realization: But that is no way for a teacher to act (in fact their progessive school teacher did not act in this way), and the little girl is no teacher.

When children turn from play and fantasy to storytelling, they try to draw their hearers together with themselves under the spell of the illusion they create. They want us to react to the situations they depict as we would to similar situations in reality, to suffer with their protagonists when they are in trouble, and to feel elated in their triumphs. A nine-year-old girl, Katherine, makes up this story. "Once upon a time there was a little poor beggar girl in the city of Paris. Everyone was rich and high, and she wondered why everyone was rich and high and she was poor. Nobody ever paid attention to her. She went to the baker's wife and asked: 'Can I have a crumb of bread?' And the baker's wife said: 'No! Amscray! No one with less than a million can have even a crumb here.' So she went to the butcher, and the butcher was very nice but his wife was very mean. And she said: 'If you give her a scrap of meat, I'll divorce you. All Paris will know.' So she went to the mayor and the mayor gave her a meal. The mayor said: 'Selsily, taste the food for her.' Selsily was the maid. And she was in the plot so the girl shouldn't have any food. She tasted it in one gulp and gave back the bones. The girl said: 'Good! Bones! I hate meat and love bread and bones.' . . . So the girl ate them and when she left told Selsily to thank the mayor. . . . And all that year they had good crops. . . . Nobody knew it—it was because of the little girl."

In this story the heroine is frustrated by a series of mother-figures who meanly withhold what the kind father-figures would give. Katherine translates the mother's monopoly of the father into terms of food to make her reproach more justifiable: the mother has no right to withhold food from the hungry child. The little girl's devouring tendencies are projected onto the mother (maid) who greedily consumes all the meat. However, the mother is outwitted; since she does not realize that what the girl wants is the bone (probably symbolizing the paternal phallus), the girl gets this prize after all. In the end, with a munificient gesture, the girl demonstrates how others ought to treat her. With saintly goodness and magical power she feeds the whole city. In her story Katherine has transformed herself into a blameless and suffering heroine who triumphs over her persecutors and returns good will for evil. She undoubtedly wants us to feel indignant at the wicked women and to pity the poor beggar girl whom they treat so unjustly.

In a joking story Katherine takes a different approach to her family problems. "Once there was a girl named Sissy and a boy named Heinie. They lived in a house made of brown stuff, and not logs I'm telling you! . . . Their mother was called BM. . . . One day they went into the woods to seek their fortune. They crawled to the mouth of the great world. . . . Mrs. BM was very unhappy at the sad turn of events because the two youngsters ran away. So she went looking for them. . . . When she found them sleeping contentedly at the bottom of the toilet and took them back and—shooosh! If you guessed everything up to now you'll guess that's the toilet flushing. And the family went to live downstairs, in a little brown house. The end." Here the tone is from the beginning quite different from that of the poor beggar girl's story. The children with their comically naughty names, "Sissy" (urine) and "Heinie" (behind), are not objects of sympathy. Katherine had previously told me that she would not like it if her younger sister called her "Sissy," "because it means coward and second you know what." "Heinie" is the name of the hero in a series of jokes very popular with children of this age; he keeps getting lost and his mother goes around asking everyone: "Have you seen my Heinie?" In her story Katherine makes both Sissy and Heinie excreta. She expresses in a joking way her early wish that her mother would throw her little sister out, flush her down the toilet. Children originally value highly their own body products and do not want to part with them. Later they learn that these products are to be despised. Children also frequently imagine that babies are born through the bowel, and equate babies with feces. Following this line of thought, Katherine says in effect: Mother was just as foolish to want to keep the baby as I used to be when I wanted to preserve my bowel movements. But the child who wants to throw out the baby readily imagines that she will be punished with a similar fate. Or the child has the fantasy that, to separate the younger one from the mother, the two children will run away from home together. This is what happens in Katherine's story. Katherine also reverses the idea that the children are the mother's excreta: the mother is also nothing but a BM. Thus she expresses the feeling: I am just as foolish to want that worthless mother as she was to keep the baby. Where in her serious story Katherine evokes

her longing for love from her parents, in the joking one
she makes light of this wish by devaluing its object.
While she wants us to be touched by the romantic suffer-
ings of her poor beggar girl, she does not expect sympathy for the sentimental relations of a family consisting
of bowel movements who live in a toilet. The joking story
is a means of repudiating the wishes that are painfully
evoked in serious fantasy. There is also less illusion of
reality in the joking story, more awareness from the start
that these are not real mothers and children.

The protagonists of a joke or comedy are less objects
of sympathy than those of a serious story or drama. This
frequently comes about through the ineptitude or inappropriate reactions of the comic protagonist: he does not
know what he is doing, does not see the hazards he risks,
and fails to react adequately to the catastrophes he undergoes. We feel that we would not behave as he does,
while his imperviousness to distress exempts us from
pity.[14] Five-year-old Ann brings out these qualities of
the comic protagonist in a story of a "silly old man": "A
man bought a watch in a store. He always buys this and
that, buys and buys and buys . . . and he didn't know
what to do with what he bought. He bought a necklace,
and he didn't know it wasn't for a man. They said, 'You
silly old man, silly old man, you never do anything reasonable.' He lost all his teeth one day. . . . He didn't have
any feelings. He said, 'I don't have any feelings. You
can do anything you want with me.' . . . He didn't know
how silly he was. . . . He didn't wear any clothes. He went
all bare in the street. . . . He got a big bruise, it was
bleeding. . . . There was nothing he could do for it. He
didn't know what he said was the silliest in the world. . . .
He used to wear a mask and stick holes in his face so no
one would know he was a man. He painted his face black.

A very silly man." This silly man anticipates the moron, the hero of the favorite jokes of children over six. The silly man in Ann's story is rash, naughty (exposing himself), and self-destructive. He undergoes and purposely produces a series of calamities which have the significance of depriving him of his masculinity. But through it all, as Ann repeats, and as the bystanders in her story affirm, he is so silly that he neither amends his ways nor realizes what has happened to him. Thus we are exempted from feeling sorry for him and are supposed to laugh at him instead. Insensitivity to damage also merges with the unvulnerability of the comic hero and the prominence in our awareness of the fact that none of this really happens.

VI

In this chapter we have seen how children use joking to transform their feelings in situations which rouse anxiety, guilt or disappointment. Joking appears as an alternative to wishfulfilling fantasies, play, and storytelling. In joking there is an interplay of the dream-like and reality-bound levels of consciousness. The magical transformation of the painful into the pleasant assumes the guise of a comic error of thought (as if one could mistake a "bier" for a "beer"). Realistic criticism is turned upon the merely wished-for or imagined: it's not real, not serious, it's just in fun (the slap-stick comedy of the boy who wrecks the house). Conflicting wishes are turned into a logical contradiction. The symbolic representation which veils the forbidden is taken literally, and by this means the tragically unattainable becomes the comically improbable (grandfather proposing marriage to a little lamb). The grandiose, the huge size which children ascribe to adults in their fantasies, and which they long to attain, is seen as an impossible exaggeration.

CHAPTER 2

Sex, Names,
and Double Meanings

I

PLAY on the ambiguity of words draws upon two basic ambiguities, those of sex and of emotion. Every individual has bisexual tendencies, and children especially feel that sex is indeterminate, that a boy could be changed into a girl or a girl into a boy. As far as emotion is concerned, every relationship partakes of some ambiguity: there is an admixture of hate in every love, and conversely love tends to infuse hostilities. These two major ambiguities of life are involved in the verbal ambiguities which are played upon in joking. It will be objected that playing on double meanings of words is a trivial amusement, incommensurate with the fateful ambiguities of sex and of emotion. This is true for adults. But this triviality is arrived at by a reduction of feelings which are originally serious and disturbing. It is the same kind of reduction as that by which the names of gods become for the unbelieving almost meaningless swear words; awesome and taboo syllables with which the supernatural was once invoked are reduced to exclamations of mild annoyance.

Everything in life at first seems invested with mysterious, wonderful, and dangerous powers. Words are weighted with magical force. The child feels that in learning the names of persons and things he gains a marvelous power over them. When he calls the name of a person, does not that person come to him? When he calls the name of a thing, is it not supplied? [15] To exchange names or to shift their meanings has at first an eerie and disturbing effect, as if in this way the things designated would themselves be transformed. Words must be divested of their magical significance before playing with them can become a joke. Then the formerly fearful, which we have found has really no terrible effect, becomes the comic.[16]

If we trace the prehistory of word play to the early playing with ambiguity which we can observe in children, we can see how it derives from the two basic ambiguities, of sex and of emotion. Both these ambiguities invest in a high degree the proper name. One's name is the mark of sexual as well as individual identity. Children's wishes to change their names often express a wish to be of the opposite sex or to have better sexual equipment. The child also learns that his name can be used lovingly or angrily: the same name seems to have exactly opposite meanings as it is used in a tender or an accusing tone of voice. It is these ambiguities of the proper name which provide the material for children's early word play.

The focus of children's word play is to begin with the proper name, which is used jokingly long before play on common names is mastered. I was struck by how often the ambiguous word in the jokes of school-age children was presented as a proper name. These proper names (in jokes which I shall analyze presently) were words of sexual or aggressive significance, turned for the purpose of the joke into names of persons, such as "Heinie,"

"Tits," "Free-show," "Fuckerfaster," "Pinch-me," "Shut-up," and "None-of-your-business." In younger children, I observed how they tended to seize on a new name and to wrest from it a meaning by which they attacked the person whose name it was. In still younger children I found a simpler form of name play; they made a joke of reassigning names, calling Johnny "Mary," and so on. When such a game was played, there was usually some child who protested at its unsettling effect, refusing to accept the changed name of himself or another. Thus one could see how taking it as a joke represented a mastery of disturbing emotions. On the youngest level to which I was able to trace word play, the joke consisted in calling a girl a boy, or a boy a girl.

I should like to trace first the line of development from the playful changing of sex and names to word play, and later to take up the kinds of jokes which derive from the ambivalent connotations of the proper name (as a love name and a bad name).

II

The joke about the change of sex was initiated in a group of three-year-old children in this way. A boy who had a new baby sister frequently asserted: "I'm a boy." No doubt he had a strong need to reassure himself on this point. The other children would sometimes retort in a teasing way: "You're a bad boy." One day the boy said to one of the little girls: "You're a boy." The girl repudiated this, saying: "Why, I don't even look like a boy." Apparently she was still too preoccupied with stabilizing her feminine identity to be able to take this proposed reversal lightly. However, from here on the idea of a sex change was taken up by the other children as a joke. According to the teacher's observation, it was the favorite joke of the group throughout the course of the year. At first the joke was apt to be enjoyed more by the initiator than by the child whose sex was allegedly changed, but in time it came to be accepted as a joke by the second child as well. Saying to a girl, "You're a boy," and to a boy, "You're a girl," represented the height of wit for these three-year-olds. It was a particularly good joke when the boy who had started it one day said to the teacher: "You're a boy." [17]

Behind this joke lay the fantasy, the wish and the fear that one's sex could be changed. Might not the assignment of the opposite sex name work a real transformation? The initial reaction was one of uneasiness. The boy who first called a girl a boy was struggling against his fear of losing his masculinity, and tried to ward it off by denying the existence of any but male creatures. The child who first laughed at the alleged sex reversal was probably the one who had achieved the most certainty about his or her sexual identity. As the playful sex switch became a generally accepted joke it meant for each child a mastery of doubts about his own sex.

One's name is a peculiarly valuable possession, the mark of one's sexual and personal identity. Before a child is born, speculations on whether it will be a boy or a girl are closely linked with the choice of a name. In the unconscious one's name may be equated with one's sexual parts. In primitive cultures the speaking of one's own name is often taboo. To utter one's name involves shameful feelings, or sometimes has a provocative effect, as if one had exposed one's genital.

The significance of the name as a promise of sexual power is found in the Bible. When God foretells to Abraham the number and greatness of his progeny, he gives him in the same breath a new name. "Behold, my covenant is with thee, and thou shalt be the father of a multitude of nations. Neither shall thy name any more be called Abram, but thy name shall be Abraham; for the father of a multitude have I made thee. And I will make thee exceedingly fruitful, and I will make nations of thee, and kings shall come out of thee." [18] And the hundred-year-old Abraham, though he laughs at what he considers an improbability, having been given a new name, becomes a father.

The loss of a name appears as a portent of castration in a humorous epic (castration, as is often the case, being here equated with total fatality). In Lewis Carroll's "Hunting of the Snark" the unfortunate hero is haunted by the prediction that he will "softly and suddenly vanish away" in an encounter with a nightmarish beast. This disaster, which eventually occurs, is anticipated by the hero's loss of his name. Having embarked on his fateful voyage, he finds that all his belongings have been left behind,

> . . . . but the worst of it was
> He had wholly forgotten his name.
> He would answer to 'Hi!' or to any loud cry,
>   Such as 'Fry me!' or 'Fritter my wig!'
> To 'What-you-may-call-um!' or 'What-was-his-name!'
>   But especially 'Thing-um-a-jig!'
> While, for those who preferred a more forcible word,
>   He had different names from these:
> His intimate friends called him 'Candle ends,'
>   And his enemies 'Toasted cheese.' [19]

The new names acquired by this luckless character suggest that he is destined to be consumed (fried, toasted, turned to a fritter) or that he has already undergone a diminution of his masculinity (the candle end representing a dwindled phallus). Thus names gained or lost can be heroically or comically prophetic of sexual triumph or catastrophe.

The equation of name and sex underlies the joking exchange of names which young children are so fond of. Exchanging names is substituted for calling a boy a girl and vice versa. Four-year-olds find exchanging names endlessly amusing. In a group of four-year-old children, a boy starts the game by switching the names of two of the children. He says to Billy, "You're Carol," and to Carol, "You're Billy." He continues, "Herbert is David," and the other children join in. The teacher's name is assigned to a girl named Susan, whereupon the teacher obligingly says, "I'm Susan," which is hailed by particularly loud laughter from the children. As often happens with these joking transformations of identity, one of the children feels threatened and affirms his own name. Having been called "Carol," he protests, "No, I'm Billy." The leader of the game assures him again that he is "Carol."

These name exchanges do not, however, necessarily coincide with sex reversals; the names of two girls or of two boys may be interchanged. The discovery of sex difference is the starting point for many explorations of similarity in difference and difference in similarity. A little boy and girl of four may take great interest in comparing the parts of their bodies which are alike; two little girls may discuss differences in the length of their hair, in their dresses or the color of their socks. In this way the sex difference is glossed over; boys and girls are alike, and children of the same sex are different. While overtones of the sex difference pervade the recognition of other likenesses and differences, a sense of individual identity is also reënforced. To the question 'Am I a boy or a girl?' is added: 'Who am I?' The joking reassignment of names plays on both these uncertainties. To be able to laugh the child must have mastered his uneasiness about both his sexual and his individual identity.

A name is a means of gaining power over its owner. In primitive cultures the real name of a baby is often concealed lest any ill-disposed person use it to do the child injury. Odysseus demonstrated in his encounter with the Cyclops how the concealment of a name could be life-preservative. He told the Cyclops that his name was "No-man." When the blinded giant cried out against him, he could only say that he had been injured by No-man, so that the other Cyclops were prevented from pursuing his attacker. The disguise of "No-man" may also be taken as a protective denial of masculinity, which made it possible for the hero to escape retribution for the blinding (castration) which he inflicted on the giant. In a bit of American folk-lore doggerel, a child, being questioned, refuses to give his right name:

> What's your name?—
> Pudden tame!
> Ask me again and I'll tell you the same.

Children's playful changing of their names is sometimes motivated by this wish for concealment. Instead of transforming others, the child here veils an important part of himself from the curiosity of a stranger. I was visiting a group of four-year-old children for the first time, and wanted to see if I had got their names right. When I came to Mary, she denied that was her name: "My name isn't Mary. I changed it to Pokey Joe." A little boy, Freddy, assured me: "And my name is Pokey Peter."

The danger of revealing one's name is played upon in a form of joking interchange used by older children. An eight-year-old girl gives me the formula: "You say to

someone, 'Can you keep a secret?' And they say, 'Yes.'
Then you say, 'What's your name?' And they tell you,
and then you say, 'You can't keep a secret because you
told me your name.' " The reproach against the one who
has been seduced into revealing his name involves the
equation of the name with the sexual parts. The child
who perpetrates the joke seems to offer mutual sexual
activity (secrets), but cheats the other into exposing himself and getting nothing in return.

III

Children often associate name changes with body transformations in joking play and humorous stories. In a
group of four-year-old girls, Jean says with an amused
expression: "I'll pull out my nose." She and two other
little girls proceed laughingly to pull out their noses, eye-
lids, and lips, and then their blouses. Bonnie says: "I'm
pulling out my stomach." Ella then pulls up her skirt
and stretches the elastic of her underpants. She and Bonnie pull at their genitals and giggle at each other. Bonnie
says: "I wouldn't like to be cut in half. No one could cut
us in half, we're too hard." As the girls become noisy, the
teacher warns them to quiet down. Jean says mockingly:
"Children are teachers and teachers are children." Bonnie
and Ella play a game of pretending to mistake the location of various body parts. One points to the side of her
head and says: "Here's my eyes." The other points to her
buttocks and says: "Here's my nose." Jean then proposes: "Let's change names. I'll be the changing names
one. You're Mr. Goosh, and you're Mr. Sloosh, and my
name is Mr. Foosh." She laughs over this and repeats it
several times. Here the children have produced a series
of joking fantasies about transforming themselves, which
ends in the changing of names. They play at extending

various body parts, expressing ideas of pregnancy and of having male organs. Pulling out the genitals may have been associated with the wish to obtain a male organ by cutting it off, since this is followed by the speculation whether the little girls themselves might (in retaliation) be cut in two. There is a joking reversal of adult and child roles (children are teachers and vice versa) which, while following the trend of the transformation fantasies, also serves to ward off adult interference with the game. Having changed themselves about so much, the little girls pretend to be confused about their body images, mistaking the location of various parts. Finally they assume strange and comical names. These are men's names, expressing their wish for a sex reversal. But as the names have a dirty slobbering sound they have the effect of mocking the envied male role.

The theme of name- and sex-reversals is developed more elaborately in a funny story by an older child, a girl of eight. Her story has as its starting point a drawing she has made of two grotesque figures in which the sex characteristics are reversed. This is expressed by giving the woman a very large head and the man such a tiny one that his features are almost invisible. The man is also very curvilinear while the woman is stiff and angular. This paradoxical couple become characters in a story. "Once upon a time there were two people. The girl's name was Billy and the man's name was Patricia. Now they lived in a very solemn town in which the children could not play— I mean, they could play, but they could not play together, the girls with the boys or the boys with the girls. The children did not like that, but it was the rule and they had to follow it. Every girl wore a pink or white or yellow or green dress, and could never, never, never, never even think of playing with boys. The boys wore either black or brown or blue polo shirts and pants. The girls could only play hopscotch, jump rope, and other girlish games like that. The boys could only play football and baseball and games like that. The houses were solemn too. Every house had a high chimney and a path, a door square like any door, and the windows were round. The smoke came out of the chimneys in circles like chains. If it didn't come out like that the people would be killed. Awful rules, aren't they? But usually it came out in ringlets. Everyone had one acre of ground with pine trees, plane trees, and they had to have roses. The town was funny though the people who lived there didn't think so. . . . One day the girls went blackberry picking and they met the boys who were going out hunting bears and deer. Soon, before they knew it, the boys were playing with the girls and the girls were playing with the boys. They played hopscotch and jump rope and the boys thought it was fun even though it was a girl's game. They both played Ring-o-Leavio. (In our school both boys and girls play it, but in that place it was only a boys' game). . . . And they came home and their mother said, 'Where have you been? Have you been playing with boys?' And the boys' fathers said, 'Have you been playing with girls?' The boys had stains of pink and white from the clothes of the girls. In that country the clothes were sticky. And the girls' clothes had brown and black on them. And they were all spanked and sent to bed, feeling very bad, without any supper."

In this fantasy, contact between the sexes leads to an exchange of sexual parts, symbolized by the colors of the boys' and girls' clothes which rubbed off on each other. The girl explained that the woman called Billy and the man called Patricia were the parents of the children in the story. Thus the parents have exchanged their sexual parts (represented by their names) in their contact with each other, but they forbid this to the children. In marriage the woman does take the man's name, which may express that she acquires a penis. In the little girl's fantasy this acquisition means taking it off the man and attaching it to oneself. Where she pictures the boys and girls exchanging sexual identities, she applies an image of mutual soiling (the partners stain each other with something sticky). Starting with a taboo on contact between the sexes, the little girl is led to elaborate a rigidly ordered society in which each detail is regulated and conformity enforced by the severest penalties. The planned society of the little girl's "solemn town" shows a striking analogy to adult fantasies of utopias and counter-utopias. From Plato to Orwell these imagined social orders have had as a major theme the interference with sexual relations.

The use of a funny name to express sexual ambiguity occurs in a humorous story by a ten-year-old girl on the theme of self-transformation. The hero is called Whi Chizzee (which is he), and is also known as W. Chizzee. He visits the witches' mountain (this was told on Halloween)—note the play on "witch" and "which"—and is instructed to get "a feather from the left wing of a pregnant owl, a hair from a bat's whisker, and a hair from a murderer's skull." If he obtains these he can make a wish and it will be granted. Thus he must collect body parts from other creatures, both male and female, triflingly small parts being substituted for more important ones. The girl spun out at some length her hero's difficulties in acquiring the needed items. The murderer who consented to give a hair turned out to be the hero's "brother seven times removed." The ingredients obtained are ground up into a potion and the hero gets his wish. He asks to be a witch and becomes a big witch with red hair and blue eyes. Still dissatisfied with himself, he changes his hair and eyes to black. Then he drinks his own potion —and dies. This story reduces to absurdity the wish for sexual transformation. As we have had occasion to note before, in humorous stories magic fails to give satisfaction.

Name-calling is another form of name change, which can be carried out in a seriously attacking or a joking way. In name-calling the victim is degraded often by stressing his lower body functions (as calling people "dog," "pig," or some other dirty animal) or connecting him with improper sexual activities of his parents ("bastard"). A favored form of name-calling in young children equates the person attacked with body-products. This is a favorite dirty joke of four-year-olds. One says to another: "You're a doody" ("duty," frequently pronounced "doody," meaning bowel movement in the bathroom language of this generation). With an admixture of mocking politeness, a child may hail someone with, "Hello, Mr. Doody." We may recall the funny story related in the preceding chapter about "Mrs. BM" and her children "Sissy" and "Heinie." The latter name equates a character with a low body part (behind). In the game of a group of four-year-old children thing-words were first substituted for proper names; after a certain stage of hilarity was reached, the thing-words were replaced by words for body parts. As I entered the room, one of the boys hailed me with: "Hello, Glue!" I replied, "Hello, Paste!" This evoked laughter from the children and was followed by an extended series of similar mutual greetings using thing-terms for names. The children then proceeded to eyes, nose, etc., culminating in "Hello, Penis! Hello, Boo-boo!"

In a more complicated form of name play there is an

attempt to discover a meaning in the name, usually as a joking attack against the person whose name it is. When the teacher introduced me to one five-year-old group, the children began to shout: "Wolf, ugh! she's a wolf!" They thus expressed in a joking way their fears of the strange adult as well as feelings or repugnance. In another group of children, some five and some six, where I was asked my name, the last syllable was played on: "Stains!" "Everything you put on you stains!" "Stains a stinkin' duty on your face!" The girl who initiated the idea of the stain, and who pictured the stain on my face, had previously noticed a mole on my forehead and expressed distress at its ugliness. She had then shown me two moles on her own neck which she evidently regarded as blemishes. Thus she found in my name (-stein, stain, stain on the face) an exposure of the physical defect which she had observed. In a six-year-old group, the teacher introduced a Mr. Rock. There were immediate cries of "What? Rot?" "Rock candy!" "Rock on your head!" Children even up to adolescence seem to play with proper names with greater avidity than they show in word-play on common names. There is a strong tendency to distort proper names in order to find a meaning by which their owners may be attacked or mockingly exposed. For eleven-year-olds, for instance, a teacher named Bernheimer becomes "Mr. Burpheimer." That such a play on names is considered extremely impolite among adults in our society contributes to the children's pleasure. Besides making fun of a particular victim, they are, with the impunity insured by their banding together, overstepping a general prohibition.

In contrast to cultures with stringent name taboos, ours provides little elaboration for the feeling that names are fraught with danger. The adult attitude that playing on people's names is impolite represents a weak vestige of feelings which in many primitive cultures make certain names (one's own or those of various relatives) unspeakable. Where such name taboos prevail the underlying feeling seems to be that uttering a name is equivalent to a forbidden (sexual or aggressive) contact with the person. The idea that changing or playing on a name has the effect of changing or exposing the person also occurs in children in our own culture. But since there is no elaborate superstructure of taboo about this, they are able to play with names in a joking way.[20] The incipient fear of the hazards of tampering with names is quickly dissipated. Instead of magical transformation, there are, one recognizes, only certain harmless emotional effects. It has been observed that a similar abatement of magical associations conditions the development of caricature.[21] Where tampering with an image was believed to work a magical transformation of the original, caricature was lacking. Comic deformation of images becomes possible when it is recognized that this only affects the feelings of the onlookers.

Where taboos attach to proper names, common names are subject to frequent changes. In many primitive cultures, the names of persons coincide with the words for common objects. If the proper name is taboo, the object called by the same name must be dealt with by a circumlocution. The tie which binds a common name to a thing yields to the superior claim of personal associations. In our culture, on the other hand, proper names are mainly dissociated from thing names. When children discover a thing name in the name of a person, it strikes them as something surprising and funny. The person is playfully transformed into the thing rather than the thing assuming the aura of the person. For us the bond between a common name and the thing it designates is firmly fixed, and not ordinarily subject to dissolution through personal associations. The unsettling of the connection between a common name and its object arouses uneasiness. Piaget has observed how children resist the suggestion of shifting or exchanging common names. They feel that the word is inseparable from the thing it denotes. A child of nine, for instance, while admitting that his brother could have been called something else, balks at the idea of calling the sun the moon and vice versa. He says that this would be wrong "because the sun can't change, it can't become smaller . . . the sun is always bigger, it always stays like it is and so does the moon." [22] Here there seems to be the underlying thought that to change the names would mean to change the things. The sun and moon, if called by each other's names, would change their identities. We may suspect that the boy's disturbance at the proposed name change derives from a concern about sexual identity: how could the sun (father) be smaller than the moon (mother)? It would mean that a man could be turned into a woman and vice versa. The same feeling, however, extends to words of less obvious symbolic significance than "sun" and "moon." Thus it would seem that we have invested the relation between common names and their objects with a trace of the taboo feeling which applies in other cultures to tampering with proper names. Conversely the fact that the magical associations of proper names are given little cultural sanction, but tend to remain a matter of private fantasy, contributes to the ease with which children can turn name play into a joke.

IV

Play on the ambiguity of common words begins with twisting the sense of what someone else has said. You say something and, by discovering an ambiguity in it, I transform its meaning to something you did not intend. This device gains its effect from the close involvement of the speaker with his words. In terms of underlying feelings, a person is what he says; to transform his meaning is to transform him. Thus play on words takes its place in the series which began with calling a boy a girl or vice versa: I change your sex; I change your name; I change your meaning. For young children the latter transformation has a similar impact to the preceding ones.

Let us observe how a word-play joke originates in a four-year-old child and how it is received by an age-mate. Several children are seated around a table with pencils and paper trying to make letters. Leonard, who is one of the most expert, keeps looking over at Bernice's letters and finding fault with them: "You made an 'E' backwards." Bernice feels quite unsettled by Leonard's criticisms (which are in fact well founded) and retorts defensively: "*You* made an 'E' backwards!" (which is not true). A moment later Bernice announces proudly: "I made a 'U'." Leonard, smiling, points at her and exclaims: "You, you, you!" Bernice reacts with intense distress: "Don't do that!" Almost in tears she appeals to the teacher: "I made a 'U' and Leonard says it's me," pointing to herself, "and it's a letter!"

In his word-play the boy has transformed the girl's image of herself, saying in effect: You're not as good as you think you are. The joking attack has arisen out of his immediately preceding criticisms of the little girl and her attempts to turn them back against him (especially with her emphatic "you"). A feeling of the boy's superiority and the girl's inadequacy has been evoked in both of them. When he then deprives what she says of its intended meaning, it carries the impact of a massive devaluation of her ambitions: she does not mean what she thinks she means; she is not what she would like to be. Just as children at first react with distress to the playful change of sex and names, so here the shift of meaning has a disturbing effect. By the change of her meaning the little girl feels deprived of something of hers that she values. In time such a playful transformation of one's meaning becomes less of a threat. One realizes that one has not really lost anything through the verbal shift, and one is able to laugh. But even with adults, if their vanity is intense or they feel very strongly about what they are saying at the moment, making a pun on what they have said may rouse annoyance rather than amusement. What Freud called "harmless wit," a play on words whose meaning is neither sexual nor hostile,[23] is thus initially not so harmless or simply pleasant. Word-play, associated in its beginnings with sex- and name-changes, has originally the force of a sexual and hostile attack, regardless of the meaning of the words involved. To accept it as harmless, we must overcome the tendency to react to it as dangerous. We are then able to laugh through an economy of emotion, as the threat of the transformed meaning ceases to affect us with its original force. The one who initiates the shift of meaning with joking intent feels that his attack is not really dangerous. He realizes that in mutilating another's meaning he is not doing any actual damage. By expressing his aggression in a joking way he reduces his anxiety about the dangerousness of his impulses.

The aggressive use of shifts of meaning may be illustrated further in the case of a five-year-old girl, who showed great cleverness in discovering ambiguities in pictures. Her teen-age brother, who was much admired in the family for his artistic skill, liked to draw pictures for her. She would then interpret them mockingly in a way he did not intend, using all her ingenuity to find in what he drew a resemblance to something other than what it was supposed to be. The boy became so offended by what he felt, quite correctly, to be a belittling reaction that he stopped making pictures for her. The changed interpretations which the little girl imposed on her brother's drawings meant that she refused to see what he was trying to show off for her admiration. She deprived his pictures of their meaning, and him of his merit. Further she asserted that what looked like one thing could be another (she could be a boy). That her wish to change her sex was a motive for her play on ambiguous appearances was evident when I drew some pictures for her. As I drew what was intended to be a picture of her, she said laughingly that the bowed upper lip looked like a moustache. The whole figure seemed to her to resemble a mermaid and she demanded that it be supplied with a tail.

In their play children change meanings and identities in a friendly and collaborative way which contrasts with the more forcible procedure of joking. For purposes of play the meaning to be assigned to an object or the role to be assumed by an individual is decided by common agreement. One child says to another: "This block will be the engine, OK?" or "We're going to play house—will you be the daddy?" And the child waits for the other to agree so that they can proceed on the basis of mutually accepted conventions. Joking, as we have seen, follows a different line: a pretended transformation is imposed on the other person without his consent. Joking resembles playful scaring in which one child surprises another with an unforeseen transformation of role, pretending to be a dangerous attacker, and where the victim (through partial mastery of fear, enjoyment of scary feelings in moderate doses, and identification with the aggressor) becomes able to react with laughter.

Children's first word-play consists in playing on some-one else's words. Later the joker himself presents both sides of the double meaning. The listener is induced to think of the first meaning and is then subjected to a re-versal of it. The joker in this way makes himself inde-pendent of the variable opportunities provided by the other person's utterances. He does not have to wait for the other to say something the meaning of which he can turn around. With the double meaning joke he makes the other assume a meaning which he then unexpectedly transforms. We have seen that the change of another person's meaning has the underlying implication: You are not what you think you are. Similarly the transfor-mation of one's own meaning suggests: I am not what you think I am. This also has initially an unsettling effect. In children's joking changes of names, those who found them disturbing often reacted with distress when a play-mate maintained he was someone else. The safe and fa-miliar person was transformed into a stranger.

The self-transformation involved in comic acting may also serve as an attack against others. Mocking imper-sonations convey a critique of their models.[24] Charlie Chaplin, in assuming the role of the little tramp, ex-pressed hostile feelings in another way. By showing him-self as helpless, tattered, and derelict, he directed a bitter reproach to the parents who had abandoned him in his childhood: Look what you have made of me! In word-play jokes the drama of self-transformation is enacted in a very small compass. But the theme is the same: I change myself (change my meaning) as an attack against some-one else. In the shift of meaning, however, something en-joyable may be revealed which compensates the hearer.

Also in the content of the joke the attack may be diverted to a third person against whom the joker and listener are allied. Finally the joking aggression may be directed against the joker himself. We shall have occasion to examine these alternatives in more detail later on.

V

We have seen how children's interest in playing with names proceeds from the joking reversal of sex and leads to more general word-play. Thus we reconstructed the series of joking transformations: I change your sex; I change your name; I change your meaning. The proper name constitutes the link between the ambiguity of sex and the wide range of verbal ambiguities. But the joking play on names, which children find so fascinating, has another major derivation. The child learns from experience that his own name can be used in two opposite ways, lovingly and angrily. The proper name itself thus possesses a double meaning.

The child first learns his own name in the course of loving interchange between himself and his mother. The mother asks: "Where's Johnny?" and points to the child, informing him: "There he is!" After a sufficient number of repetitions, the child succeeds in responding to the question, "Where's Johnny?" by pointing to himself. The mother is delighted with his achievement, hugs and kisses him, and repeats, "Yes, there he is!" Thus the child feels that he acquires a separate identity (symbolized by his name), only as a prelude to a complete and loving reunion with the mother, in which he hopes to recapture with intensified pleasure his earlier sense of fusion with her. This expectation is inevitably disappointed. The mother fails to gratify the child's longings for physical love, and indeed prohibits to a large extent his strivings in this direction. His name, originally a love name, assumes an aura of mingled feelings, regret and frustration as well as love and pride. Then he also learns that his name can be used in a sharply negative way: "Johnny Jones! What have you been doing!" His name now underscores a reprimand. The tone of voice in which it is uttered turns it into a bad name. "Johnny Jones!" called out in that angry and reproachful way clearly means: You're a bad boy. The child thus has two names: the love name and the bad name. His name is ambiguous, its meaning depending on the mother's tone of voice.[25]

Both the love name and the bad name provide themes for jokes. The name of a child-figure may be turned into a means of retaliation against the adult. The love name serves to obtain sexual gratification from the withholding mother or to expose her against her will. The child wrests from the mother in a forcible and mocking way the satisfactions which the love name first seemed to promise.[26] There is a series of jokes, very popular with children of about nine, which deal with a mother and her child named "Heinie" (behind). The following is typical: Heinie gets lost and the mother asks a policeman: "Have you seen my Heinie?" The policeman replies: "No, but I'd sure like to." There are endless variations. The mother buys Heinie some ice-cream, which he gets smeared over his face. The mother then asks the man behind the counter: "Can I have a tissue for my Heinie?" The mother goes to a shoe store and says: "I want a pair of shoes for my Heinie." Through some far-fetched mishap, Heinie at a fiesta gets suspended by a lasso from a balcony and the mother cries: "Oh, my Heinie is hanging over the bannisters!"

By setting up a situation in which the mother calls the child "my Heinie," the loving union of child and mother is achieved in a mocking way: the child becomes again a part of the mother's body. The mother in the joke does not know what she is saying, just as in actuality she did not acknowledge the wishes she evoked by the love name. While the mocking love name accomplishes a symbolic fusion of mother and child, the action of the joke consists in the mother's unwitting self-exposure. Her concern for her child keeps impelling her to reveal an intimate part of her body. This is just what the child would have wished, but the mother in actuality was not so compliant. The joke places her in a predicament where she exposes herself without realizing what she is doing. Involuntary self-exposure regularly has a comic effect; the person appears to have made a foolish mistake in letting down his guard.[27] Such a person becomes not only a source of unexpectedly easy gratification for the onlooker, but also an object of disparagement. Thus the mother in the joke is exposed as both sexually accessible and foolish. She is punished for having been so withholding. Her image is degraded; from having been ideally desirable she becomes ridiculous. In the joke it is usually to a man that the mother offers herself, as when she asks the policeman: "Have you seen my Heinie?" This conveys the further reproach against the mother for yielding to the father what she denies to the child. The child wonders how the forbidding mother can indulge in sexual activity. The joke represents her as not knowing what she is doing.

In another joke, a woman has a dog named "Tits." The dog's ball rolls away, and the woman hands the dog to a man, saying: "Will you hold my Tits while I go and get the ball?" (I should guess that there was originally a double word-play in this joke, implying that the woman also holds the man's balls, but the nine-year-old boy who told it to me apparently had not caught this.) Here the

child, represented by the dog, is again identified through
his name with a part of the mother's body, this time merging with the breast. The mother unwittingly exposes herself by using the child's name and offers herself to a man
under the guise of solicitude for her child. There is an
irony in this, since the child feels that if the mother loved
him as much as she pretends she would not give herself to
the father.

In a similar joke, the child's name is a signal for the
mother's total body exposure. A woman has a little dog
named "Free-show." While the woman is taking a bath,
the dog runs out of the house. The woman jumps up and
runs out after the dog calling, "Free-show! Free-show!"
And, as a nine-year-old girl explained, "All the people
thought she meant it was a free show." Here the child
(dog) evidently resents the mother's excluding him from
the bathroom. He withdraws from her in turn, runs away,
and thus induces the wished-for exhibition of the mother,
again by the use of his name.

When the mother calls the child's name in the following
joke she directly incites him to sexual activity. As told by
an eleven-year-old boy: "There was this guy named
Johnny Fuckerfaster. In school one day he did something
wrong and the teacher told him to stay after school. Everyone was dismissed and he said to the teacher, 'Take off
your socks.' It was a French teacher. And he said, 'Take
off your girdle, take off your underwear.' Finally she was
all undressed. And his mother came looking for him and
she called him: 'Johnny Fuckerfaster! Johnny Fuckerfaster!' And he was over by the teacher, and he thought
she meant 'fuck her faster.' And his mother called him
again and he said: 'Mom, I'm fucking her as fast as I
can.'" Here the child's name resumes its early associations as an inducement to love, though the mother does not

mean to use it in this sense. The mother is given a double representation; she unwittingly stimulates amorous impulses in the child by calling his name, and, as the teacher, she gratifies these impulses. The teacher's being French accounts for her sexual freedom, and also affirms her remoteness from the incestuous object. By means of these two complementary figures, the forbidding mother is transformed into one who makes excessive sexual demands on the child.[28] It is not the child who wants too much from the mother, but she who requires more than a little boy can perform. As in the Heinie jokes, the withholding mother is mockingly exposed as too easy and eager.

The exaction of love from a presumably unwilling object, combined with hostility towards the object, is expressed in the following joke which works with changes of identity rather than with names. A ten-year-old girl instructs me: "Whatever kind of lock I say I am, you say you're that kind of a key. I'm a gold lock." "I'm a gold key." "I'm a silver lock." "I'm a silver key." . . . "I'm a don lock." "I'm a don key." The child here transforms herself into a female sex symbol and asks the other person to become the corresponding male symbol. Through a series of transformations (gold, silver, etc.) they remain inseparable partners. This is a love fantasy. But it is not the real thing, and in the end the resentment for present and past frustrations asserts itself. The partner is tricked into confessing he is a donkey. In effect: You don't really love me—what a fool you are! The withholding person is punished by being devalued.

The bad name also provides a theme for jokes. The hostile associations which the child's name has acquired in reprimands are turned back against the adult. The name which has been used scoldingly against the child is transformed into a hostile retort. Here is a joke of this kind which I heard repeatedly from children between the ages of seven and nine. As an eight-year-old boy tells it: "Once upon a time there were two boys, one named Shut-up and the other named Trouble. And they were walking out one day and Shut-up got lost. And he went to the police station and the policeman asked him his name so he said 'Shut-up.' So the policeman thought—you see he said 'Shut-up' because his name was Shut-up. So the policeman said: 'Are you looking for trouble?' You see Trouble was the other boy's name. And he said 'Yes.' Get the trick?" In other versions the first boy's name is "None-of-your-business" or "Mind-your-own-business." The narration may be prolonged by having the policeman question the boy repeatedly, bring him before the judge for further questioning and so on, so that the boy can say "Shut-up" or "Mind-your-own-business" many more times.

When the grown-ups scold the child, he feels that they are cutting him off from contact with them. His name, called out angrily, seems equivalent to "Shut up!" or "Mind your own business!" The child's name in the joke is thus transformed into its bad meaning. A situation is contrived in which this bad name can be turned back against the adults. When they ask his name, as grown-ups so often ask a child, he retorts with the bad name. It becomes a means of retaliation; the adults' aggression boomerangs. There is also mocking compliance in the child's response. In saying "Shut up" to the policeman, the representative of punishing authorities, the child is only answering his question; implicitly he is only repeating the bad name that has been given him. The rebellious and critical child feels that the adults indulge their hostility against him while demanding that he inhibit the corresponding feelings in himself. The joke gives him an

opportunity to reply in kind, with the justification that
they have asked for it. The two children, "Shut-up" and
"Trouble," are sometimes made explicitly two brothers
or a brother and a sister. One boy who told me the joke
remarked immediately afterwards that his little sister is
a lot of trouble. When the two children in the joke wander
off and one loses the other, the child has got rid of the
troublesome sibling. This is the naughtiness for which
the authorities are reproaching him. The child replies in
effect that it is all their fault for having had another
child, and that he is not his brother's keeper.

Starting with his painful awareness of his parents' ambivalence towards him, as they are sometimes loving
and sometimes angry, the child is quick to observe the in-
consistency of their behavior towards other people as well.
He overhears what the parents say between themselves
about the guests whom they have invited with such demon-
strations of friendliness, and he sometimes discomfits his
parents by repeating their strictures to the company. In
the following joke children parody the grown-ups' politeness which they understand often conceals hostility. A
child pretends to introduce himself, saying: "My name is
Cliff. Why don't you drop over some time?" Or, "My
name is East River. Why don't you drop in some time?"
(I heard these from six-year-olds.) The children have
understood that underneath the courteous interchanges
of grown-ups there may be the suppressed wish to say:
Go jump in the lake! This ambivalence is again conveyed
through the medium of the name, with its potentiality for
expressing positive and negative feelings.

VI

We have seen how the ambiguity of words, the major
resource of verbal joking, derives its effect from two basic

ambiguities: those of sex and of emotion. For the child the two crucial questions, 'Am I a boy or a girl?' and 'Am I loved or hated?' give an aura of ambiguity to his name. His name is the mark of his sexual identity, but might it not be changed? After playing quite simply at calling a boy a girl and vice versa, children turn to the game of changing names. As the unsettling loss of identity ceases to be frightening, it becomes a joke. The child's name also has the ambiguity of being a love name or a bad name depending on whether the parents are affectionate or scolding. In jokes revolving around the love name, the intimacy withheld by the mother is mockingly extorted. The bad name is used in a similar way to retaliate against the parents; the aggression which they have expressed against the child boomerangs. Again we see, as in the preceding chapter, how joking provides a rectification of painful experiences. In so far as the child has been disappointed in connection with the love name which he has been called and has found the bad name unbearable, his twisting of others' meanings implies: I will get from what you say something I like better than what you intend. A gratifying sexual meaning is read in, or a way is found to turn the words into an attack against the speaker. These devices, which for children so often remain bound to the original context of the proper name, are capable of extension to every utterance. It is only as a result of long development that we can take some verbal communications impersonally. To begin with, every word that is addressed to us is felt as either gratifying or painful. For the child every word that he receives from the adults has to some degree the same emotional significance as that which attaches to his own name: it can be a promise of gratification or a rebuke. From this we may derive the impulse to play on words, to extract a forbidden (withheld) sexual meaning or to bring out and redirect against others the hostility which was felt to be implicit in their words.

The ambiguities which attach to the proper name are extended to common words also by virtue of the feeling of identity of the person with what he says. To transform the meaning of what a person says has for children originally the impact of transforming the other person's sex or identity against his will. What a person is and what he means are taken as the same thing; hence such word play signifies: You are not what you think you are. We have seen how young children initially regard the playful change of their sex, or identity, or meaning as an attack. In the course of development, it gets to be understood on both sides that no real transformation is worked by these verbal shifts. The willful change, divested of magical force, becomes a joke.

Word play has for children originally an aggressive and sexual significance. To distort another's meaning is to transform him radically since what he means and what he is are the same. It is only as particular utterances become to some extent isolated from the total personality, so that one does not cease to be oneself if one's meaning is inverted, that play on words becomes harmless. The original impact of word play is then restored by the infusion of a sexual or aggressive content. For adults the "U—you" joke of the four-year-old could not have such a devastating impact. To recapture the earlier effect of word play we must find more overt aggression or sex in the words themselves.

As early feelings about word play become attenuated, it assumes the harmless quality which suits it to be a façade for sexual or hostile joking. There is a concurrence of two lines of development in the production of the complex joke form which uses word play as a façade. There is the progressive and drastic reduction of the original disturbance about shifts of meaning, which we have discussed in this chapter. Concurrently increasing inhibitions against sexual and aggressive impulses are instituted which require their masking by the joke façade (a development which I shall analyze in Chapter 4). Word play having become harmless, is then utilized for this purpose.

CHAPTER 3

Riddles
and the Legend
of the Moron

I

THE joking riddle is the favorite form of joke for children between the ages of six and eleven. The child who asks the riddle shows how smart he is, for when the other cannot guess, he gives the answer himself. A great number of these riddles have to do with the behavior of a moron, someone who does stupid things that the child would not do. In contrasting himself with the moron, the child again feels how smart he is. Children at this age are peculiarly preoccupied with the issue of who is smart and who is dumb. They are especially sensitive to being put in the wrong or not knowing what someone else knows. When a child has been outwitted or outdone by another, one hears the heartfelt cry: "You think you're smart!" Any advantage is apt to be felt as smartness, any disadvantage as dumbness. This preoccupation is reflected in the favored jokes of children of this age. The riddle form stresses the issue of who knows and who doesn't. The fig-

ure of the moron represents all that the child repudiates
in his aspirations to smartness.

With striking punctuality children seem to acquire a
store of joking riddles at the age of six. As one six-year-
old girl remarked: "We didn't know any of these jokes
last year." At six and seven about three times as many
joking riddles are told as jokes in any other form. In the
following three years the percentage of riddles is a little
over half. At eleven and twelve it is reduced to a third;
riddles are being discarded in favor of anecdotes.[29] Children from six to eleven are apt to use the terms "riddle"
and "joke" interchangeably. Asked to define a riddle a
seven-year-old boy says: "If people have riddles—like
the moron jokes. Jokes are riddles." Similarly a seven-
year-old girl: "Something funny, something like a joke."
Asked to define a joke: "Something very funny. The same
thing as a riddle, a joke is." Another seven-year-old girl
has defined a riddle as "something somebody has to
guess." When asked later what a joke is, she says: "I told
you before. It's something you tell the answer to." A seven-
year-old boy says that riddles are "things that people like
to say. It spreads a lot of good cheer and laughter." This
equation of riddles with jokes may continue up to the
age of eleven. Thus an eleven-year-old girl says that a
riddle is "like a joke, the same thing as a joke." And
conversely, a joke is "like a riddle, another thing that
would make you laugh." While some children from about
eight on are able to distinguish in their definitions between jokes and riddles, when asked to tell jokes they
almost without exception tell joking riddles.

The joking riddle deals with knowledge in a special
way: it makes a parody of questions and answers. The
question posed is trivial or absurd; the solution is nonsensical. In the period of their lives preceding the age of

six, children have experienced intense sexual curiosity, which has remained incompletely satisfied. Even the most modern parents have inevitably frustrated and disappointed the child, not letting him see for instance all that he would like to see, much less gratifying his sexual longings which go beyond seeing. Often they have seemed to give foolish or evasive answers to his questions. With the onset of what Freud has called the "latency period," at about six, much of the earlier sexual preoccupation undergoes repression, to be revived again at puberty. The impulse to know is normally sublimated into more impersonal investigations, into the acquisition of school learning. But may we not expect to find some emotional reaction to the chagrin and disappointment in which the curiosity of the earlier phase ended? I think we find it in the joking riddles.

In joking riddles children make fun of their earlier investigations, substituting silly questions and answers for the serious ones of the past. The knowledge they sought and the parents who gave them unsatisfactory answers are subjected to mockery. It is as if the child says to the parents: that is the kind of nonsensical answer you gave me. He can also disparage the secrets he was unable to discover. In the riddle something is concealed, there is something hard to guess, but when the answer is produced it turns out to be absurd. The child can overcome his chagrin at not knowing by exposing others' ignorance. He asks other children his riddles and proves they are dumb for not knowing the answers. At this age the child has displaced a considerable part of the love, hate, and rivalry which he originally felt towards the parents to other children. By outdoing them he can rectify the disadvantage he experienced before. In the joking riddle the child can express his mixed feelings about knowing and also circumvent its hazards. He has come to feel that the knowledge he sought was too dangerous. By means of the riddle he demonstrates that he knows something but disguises it as foolish, that is, harmless. We shall see that the joking riddles conceal meanings related to the child's earlier sexual investigations. These latent meanings account for the children's addiction to seemingly trivial witticisms. But the meaning remains disguised most of the time. The joking riddles differ from the sort of dirty joke where what looks at first harmless is shown to have a sexual significance. In the riddles what looks harmless at the beginning is apt to look the same way at the end.

The riddle is a purely verbal formula. As such it is a model of non-empirical knowledge. One knows something without having looked. In this respect also it is of great value to the latency period child who wants to free himself from the guilt of his previous investigations in which forbidden looking, or the longing to see forbidden things, played a prominent part.

II

In folklore and mythology riddle-solving and looking have opposite results. Knowing without looking, in solving a riddle, is rewarded; looking is punished. The hero or heroine who can answer a riddle overcomes terrible dangers and gains all that his heart desires. In contrasting plots the protagonist is forbidden to look at something, but cannot resist the temptation and so provokes catastrophe. Oedipus overcame the Sphinx by answering her riddle: what is it that walks on four legs in the morning, two legs at noon, and three legs at night? The answer was: man. In infancy he crawls on four legs, in his prime he walks on two legs, in old age he hobbles with a cane. By giving this answer Oedipus escaped the penalty of death which the Sphinx imposed on all who failed to solve her riddle, and proceeded to his fateful triumph becoming king in Thebes and marrying the queen. The riddle in its latent meaning deals with the intercourse of the parents as observed by the child. The father is on all fours, the mother's two legs are outstretched, the third leg is the penis which appears and disappears.[30] But this view is concealed in the manifest riddle where there appears instead a single person, man, the son in isolation from the parents. (We shall see that in the moron riddles a similar disguise is used. While the latent content deals with the sexual activity of the parents, on the manifest level we find the moron-child alone.) Oedipus triumphed in his claim to know without having looked, to be concerned only with knowing himself, and to have freed himself from the wishes roused by his childhood observations of his parents. But it was his fate to know in the fullest and most forbidden sense, to have sexual knowledge of his mother. When at last he learned that the queen he had married was his mother, his despairing cry was, "I have seen too much!" and he tore out his eyes. Thus the immunity provided by knowing in a riddling, non-seeing way broke down; the other kind of knowing was not averted.

Jesus died after he failed to answer the riddle asked by Pilate: "What is truth?" While Pilate's question on the manifest level appears to be rhetorical, from its place in the pattern of the hero myth, as well as from its profound significance, it may be taken as a riddle by which the hero is tested. In Jesus the taboo on knowing in the sense of carrying out the oedipal wishes, had been observed to the fullest extent. Jesus had completely renounced both sex and aggression. Thus in contrast to Oedipus he could not answer the riddle with which he was confronted at a crucial moment in his career, and he perished. In both these stories, knowing the answer to the riddle turns out to be inseparable from dangerous sexual knowledge. Hence one inevitably knows either too much or too little. The one who has renounced forbidden knowledge cannot answer the riddle; the one who can answer the riddle, through the knowledge already provided by his forbidden impulses, will be driven further by them, to disaster. The wish of the riddle-solver to have knowledge but escape its hazards is denied.[31]

In fairy tales, however, where fatalities are more often circumvented than in myths, the answering of a riddle may be wholly saving. In "Rumpelstiltskin," the young queen who is able to guess the name of the little dwarf destroys him and can keep her baby. She knows the answer without having carried on investigations herself. A servant has done the spying for her, having discovered the secret hiding place of the little man in the forest, and overhearing the song in which he revealed his name. In another of Grimm's fairy tales, "The Riddle," a wicked princess challenges young men to ask her a riddle which she will not be able to answer. If she guesses the answer, the man is killed; if she cannot guess, she will marry him. A prince asks a riddle which baffles her. So she sends her maid to his bedroom at night in the hope that he will give away the answer by talking in his sleep. The maid is outwitted by the prince's servant. Finally the princess herself undertakes the nocturnal spying. Though she gets the answer to the riddle, her spying is proved against her and she loses the contest.

The fatal danger of looking is a theme of many stories. Lot's wife violated the prohibition against looking back at the cities of the plain, and was turned to a pillar of salt. Pandora could not resist looking into the closed box, and released all the troubles of the world. Orpheus, on the upward path from Hades, failed to comply with the admonition not to look at Eurydice, and so lost her forever. Bluebeard's wife, though forbidden to look into the secret closet, could not restrain her curiosity, and narrowly escaped the grisly death of which she caught an awful glimpse.

From these various stories we learn that there are two kinds of knowing, the riddling kind which is purely verbal and thus safe, and the kind which involves forbidden looking and terrible hazards. This is one of the reasons why riddles appeal to children; they represent a way of knowing without the dangers of investigation. Older children are apt to say about a riddle that if you think about it you can usually figure out the answer. No external observation is necessary; you get the answer from inside your own head. Younger children frequently deny having learned the riddle and say they always knew it.[32] The child asserts his independence in this way. Nobody told him; he knows these things by himself. But he is also maintaining that he did not to have to do any spying to find out what he knows.

Children are also apt to believe that the riddles have always existed. They deny the occurrence of the creative act by which something came into being. On the unconscious level the creative act which they deny is the sexual one which was the object of their curiosity. Thus, 'I always knew it,' and 'It always existed,' mean: I did not look, and besides nothing happened.[33] A nine-year-old boy raises the question of who made up all the moron riddles. But he hastily retreats from this overbold approach to the problem of origination: "They got them out of books, I guess." An eleven-year-old boy admits some joke production but assumes a large body of pre-existent models:

"People think they are funny and keep on making them up. The majority of jokes are moron jokes. They make up some more. A man tells his friend and the friend tells his cousin till it's all over the United States." Thus he shifts from the question of origination to the safer one of verbal transmission. A ten-year-old boy substitutes for pre-existence creation by a father at some remote time. He wonders who made up the moron jokes, and thinks: "Probably a man who had a family, and they were very joyous, and he made up these jokes for them. And they came down through the ages."

III

The way in which joking riddles serve as a continuation, a disguise, and a parody of the child's inquiries about the parents appears in the case of an eleven-year-old boy. Stephen is exceptionally fond of telling and inventing joking riddles. He and his mother make up riddles together; as he puts it, "I usually give her an idea and she dresses it up." Stephen's riddling expresses his unsatisfied curiosity about what goes on between his parents, which is intensified by frequent quarrels between them. In riddles he not only disguises the questions he does not dare to ask more directly, but he also wards off his mother's probing curiosity about him. The mother has repeatedly complained to Stephen's teachers that he does not confide in her, that when she questions him he is resentful and seems to feel attacked. As the mother is on bad terms with the father, her demand for intimate confidences from the boy probably expresses the wish to get from him the emotional satisfaction she lacks. It is not surprising that the boy feels this demand as a threat.

Mother and son turn their mutually frustrated curiosity into a game of joking questions and answers. Here is a riddle on which they collaborated: "What does a mother at a birthday party have in common with the Kefauver Committee?—They're always after the racketeer." Stephen says that his father was especially interested in the Kefauver investigations, which were prominent in the news at this time. If we take this association to indicate that the Kefauver Committee stands for the father, the underlying meaning of the riddle becomes: What does mother have in common with father? This is indeed a pressing question for the boy, especially as he has reason to think his parents may separate. Since he does not dare to ask it more openly and may doubt whether he would get a truthful answer, he expresses it in a joking riddle.

Another riddle in which Stephen is particularly interested asks: "Why did the moron put the television set on the stove?" One may suppose that the moron has seen something that enraged him. The answers suggest that he would have liked to see still more, and also indicate that it is a man against whom his destructive rage is directed. "Because he wanted to see Milton Boil.—Because he wanted to see Arthur Godfrey.—Because he wanted to see Hopalong Cassidy ride the range." It would seem that this riddle in its latent meaning deals with the child's observation of the parents, his frustration at not seeing everything, his jealous fury against the father, and the vindictive wish that his sexual heat should consume him utterly (the latter particularly in the image of God frying). Other riddles express Stephen's comparison of himself with his father, and his feeling of being overwhelmed at the size of his father's penis. For instance, "What is the longest pencil in the world?—Pennsylvania." He is also preoccupied with a riddle about how a man can get out of a locked house, to which he has a number of solutions, and which expresses among other things fear of the encompassing woman and anxiety about how the man, having entered her, can ever extricate himself. It may also express his feeling of being too closely confined with his mother and his wish to escape.

The way in which Stephen turns his conversation with his mother into a propounding of joking riddles is like a parody of the scene in which Hamlet questioned his mother in her bedroom; there also crucial questions remained unanswered. In Stephen's case we see particularly how the child uses riddling not only to pursue his questions but guard his secrets. Before his addiction to riddles, Stephen was inclined to "put an antic disposition on" in cruder ways. In school his behavior tended to be crazy and incomprehensible. He threw things around and shouted nonsense syllables. The joking riddles represent a later development of this self-concealment behind a façade of nonsense.

Children have ambivalent feelings about the joking riddles. On the one hand these riddles represent knowledge, on the other, they are a mocking substitute for more serious inquiries. Stephen expresses this when, despite his pride in knowing and inventing so many riddles, he calls them stupid. He calls a riddle "a stupid joke. Most of them are stupid. People who make them up are stupid. . . . When you make them up you feel you're being stupid. The answer is a stupid thing." Thus he expresses how in the joking riddle his pressing curiosity and pride in knowing are counterbalanced by a sense of defeat in his investigations and by his need for disguise. The riddle maker feels stupid: he is constrained to play the fool to conceal himself from his mother. The answer is a stupid thing: he has been unable to learn what he really wanted to find out.

As the joking riddle expresses the impulse to investigate under the disguise of foolishness, children are often uncertain whether it is an item of knowledge or something silly. They shift back and forth between whether it is hard or easy and whether it is funny. Asked whether she can tell me some jokes, some things that she thinks are funny, a seven-year-old girl says: "Some of the moron jokes are funny. Not exactly kind of funny—hard. Do you want to answer?" She is thus undecided whether these riddles are jokes or difficult problems. But there is also the feeling that if it is not hard it is not a good joke either. Another seven-year-old girl remarks about a riddle the answer to which she considers too obvious: "That's not funny at all. Are there some people who don't know it? Such an easy joke. I don't know why I said it was a joke." This tendency to confuse the funniness of a joke with the value of the knowledge conveyed is not peculiar to children nor related only to joking riddles. Freud observed about wit generally that it is very difficult to determine how much of our pleasure derives from the wittiness of the expression, how much from the value of the thought expressed.[34] When insights are expressed in a witty way their merit may be overestimated because of the charm of the formulation. But also the significance or shocking effect of what is revealed may be minimized by its being expressed as a joke.

In asking their riddles children engage in a mutual examination. The questioning of the parents, which we saw in the case of Stephen, is mainly redirected to agemates. The objects of earlier curiosity are replaced by safer ones. Moreover, the emphasis is more on the child's exhibition of himself than on his wish to observe. The one who asks the riddle demands that the other show whether he has the answer. But he expects to demonstrate that the other lacks it, and so to be able to exhibit the fact that he has it. On the unconscious level this stands for a comparison of sexual equipment, in which the riddler wants to show his superiority. He justifies his exhibition by forcing the other to ask for it. The chagrin of the child who does not know, and his resentment at having his inadequacy exposed, is assuaged by his being given the answer. Something is revealed to him that he can enjoy and something is given him which he in turn can use. He will have the chance to exhibit himself to advantage when he asks someone else the riddle he has just learned. The unpleasant impact which such exchanges may have was expressed by a seven-year-old girl: "I don't think jokes are funny, because when I say them over and over they get boring. And it isn't funny the first time because people are telling them to me." This child apparently found it particularly painful to be at the receiving end and was unable to accept the compensatory gratification of retelling. However, for most children the rewarding aspect of such interplay seems to outweigh the unpleasantness. The joking character of the riddle further reduces the resentment of the child who did not know the answer, since it implies on the part of the riddler: what I know, what I have, what I show you is really something silly.

IV

Let us proceed to analyze a number of the joking riddles. I was told these jokes over and over again by children from the age of six on. From the adult point of view these jokes are rather impactless. But the children seem endlessly preoccupied with them. As we uncover the latent meaning of these jokes we shall see that they deal continually with the topic of the child's earlier sexual investigations. This accounts in part for their strong appeal. But the form of the joke which conceals this significance behind a harmless façade is equally important.

The latency period child is concerned with repressing his sexual urges and curiosity, and can satisfy them only under a disguise.

Here is one of the most frequently told joking riddles:

> Why did the moron tiptoe past the medicine cabinet?
> Because he didn't want to wake the sleeping pills.

The tiptoeing and sleeping suggest that this has something to do with nocturnal investigations. The children give us a clue when they say, in explaining why this joke is funny: "Sleeping pills put you to sleep. They don't sleep themselves." The same thing could be said about the parents at night. Thus there is here what we might call a latent riddle: Why are the parents at night like sleeping pills? The moron in the joke is a fool because he doesn't know that they put you to sleep and don't sleep themselves. But is he such a fool? Why is he tiptoeing? Perhaps he knows after all that they are not asleep and is tiptoeing around to find out what really happens. The moron represents the child both in not knowing something and also, insofar as he knows, playing dumb.

Another joking riddle, an old one which I heard in my childhood, and which is still current among children today, is the following:

> What's black and white and red all over?
> A newspaper.

This harmless sounding joke also conceals a latent riddle. The clue lies in the word "red" which carries an allusion to blushing. The use of "red" in overtly dirty jokes suggests this. Here is one told by a nine-year-old girl: "What made Miss Tomato turn red?—She saw Mr. Green Pea." And another, told by an eleven-year-old boy: "Why are

fire engines red?—Wouldn't you be if your hose was always hanging out?" (There are also a number of harmless answers to the fire engine riddle, for instance, "Because they're always Russian.") If we take red in the
sense of blushing, then "black and white and red all over"
may be a naked person: the hair is black, the skin is white,
and he or she turns red all over from the shame of being
exposed. Thus we may construct the latent riddle: 'Why
is a naked person like a newspaper?' In the manifest riddle the newspaper is substituted for the naked person,
and the sublimated form of looking in newspaper reading
replaces cruder voyeurism. (That newspaper reading retains some of the emotional overtones of peeping is suggested by the prim motto of the *New York Times:* "All
the news that's fit to print." The danger that the sublimated impulse of the reader may revert to its more elementary form is guarded against by the publisher's showing only what is seemly.) In the newspaper riddle, as in
the one about the medicine cabinet, we find beneath the
harmless façade the theme of forbidden looking.

The combined themes of forbidden looking and exhibition, sex difference, and castration danger enter into the
formation of the following familiar and simple sounding
riddle:

> Why does the fireman wear red suspenders?
> To hold his pants up.

The latent meanings are suggested by children's associations. Frequently they think of the alternative of the
pants falling down. Thus a six-year-old boy says: "It
would be funny if he didn't wear red suspenders and his
pants would fall down, wouldn't it?" A seven-year-old
girl says: "Of course to hold his pants up! What do you
think? To make his pants fall down?" A five-year-old boy

after giving his own versions of the suspender riddle ("Why does everyone wear suspenders?" and "Why does the farmer wear suspenders to cross the street?") produced the following fantasy which he considered very funny: "Nobody should wear clothes. Everybody in the American world should go inside and outside without clothes." To these children the idea of pants being held up suggests the opposite. But if the pants come down then the sex difference is revealed. Or, on the more superficial level, where sex differences may be represented by differences of clothing, the wearing or not wearing of suspenders in itself differentiates boys and girls. Several children maintain, apropos of this joke, that everyone wears suspenders. This represents an attempt to deny the sex difference. A nine-year-old girl says: "Everyone wears suspenders to hold their pants up." She immediately corrects this wishful distortion: "At least I don't. It depends on whether it's underpants or top pants." In a further line of association the revelation of the sex difference evokes the danger of castration. An eight-year-old boy is led to think of robbers (castrators): "Why don't they have gangster pictures on the suspenders? Then they could really hold your pants up." Another boy introduces the idea of protection (implicitly against castration). Explaining the "trick" of the joke, he says: "People think red is a protection color. They get all mixed up."

We may further interpret "red suspenders" in terms of the allusion of "red" to blushing. The suspenders hold up the pants and prevent exposure. But if they failed to do so, the victim of exposure would turn red. The red suspenders thus represent a condensation of two opposite ideas: exposure and its prevention. As we have seen the children (though not apparently using the clue of redness) make this association of opposites. However, the sexual meaning, of the exposure with its related gratifications and anxieties, is not manifest in the telling of the joke.

This form of joke in which the latent meaning is never overtly expressed (unlike the dirty joke where the sexual meaning, at first concealed, becomes apparent) probably has a reassuring effect for the children. The dangers suggested in the latent meaning, of exposure, forbidden looking, confronting the sex difference and the possibility of castration, do not materialize. The suspenders hold up the pants. While the manifest content thus maintains the defense against the underlying thoughts, their gratifying possibilities may still be enjoyed in a secret and unacknowledged way. The exclusion of these thoughts from the manifest content of the joke may account for the relative ease with which these jokes are remembered. The common tendency to forget jokes seems related to the fact that the joke makes conscious thoughts which are usually repressed. This release from repression is only momentary. Subsequently the forbidden thoughts, and the joke which gave them expression, are again excluded from consciousness.[35] Jokes like the suspender riddle, however, keep the forbidden thoughts latent throughout. As a result they are probably less subject to forgetting. Latency period children, whose jokes are largely of this sort, are apt to have a very good memory for jokes. Unlike older children and adults, who frequently protest that their minds go blank when they are asked to recall jokes, latency period children tend to produce with great facility numerous jokes of the kind we have been dealing with.

The avoidance of dangerous thoughts is particularly evident in joking riddles where the answer is surprisingly obvious as in the case of the suspenders. The teller of the riddle suppresses or represses his own dangerous thoughts behind the harmless answer which he substitutes for them. The child can in this way also fool the adult, putting on a bland façade of innocence. A further gratification comes from disappointing the hearer, who has expected something more, making him feel foolish, and on a deeper level guilty for having begun to think of more dangerous possibilities, and for having missed the obvious because of the tendency to probe more deeply which has been stimulated. Another stock riddle which illustrates these points is:

Why did the chicken cross the road?
To get to the other side.

The associations of the children reveal the fantasies of destruction which have been warded off by the harmless answer. A seven-year-old girl says: "When I was a little girl I used to say, 'Because he didn't want the cow to eat him.'" Similarly an eleven-year-old boy who has not heard it before guesses: "Cause the cow was coming?" Others think of the chicken's being run over. An eight-year-old boy guesses: "Because it wanted to get killed? . . . How could it cross with so many cars going by?" Another eight-year-old boy says: "It's silly not funny. Why would it want to cross the road to get to the other side? It could of flew instead of getting hit by a car." A nine-year-old girl suggests: "Maybe because it wanted to kill itself?" [36] Similarly a ten-year-old boy when asked the analogous riddle, "Why did the moron cross the street and never cross back?" says: "Because he got run over. Right?" These are answers which are apt to occur to the children if they do not know the riddle. The appeal of the correct answer then derives in part from its cloaking these thoughts. We may add that being run over appears in dreams as a symbol of intercourse.[37] This meaning probably also enters into the children's fantasies about the fate of the chicken.

Children of around seven and eight are fond of inventing riddles of this kind. If we are able to observe the context in which these inventions occur, we can sometimes see what thoughts the child conceals behind the non-committal answer. A seven-year-old girl is expressing some reflections about babies. She has no younger brothers or sisters and says that she is glad of it. Small children are a nuisance and besides very worrisome. For instance they are likely to run into the street and be run over by busses. She then thinks up the following riddle: "Why does a bus have wheels?—To run, of course." Thus she diverts her own thoughts from the idea of busses running over little children, and at the same time denies to the adult the destructive thoughts which she has just revealed.

The theme of concealed investigations recurs in the following riddle:

> What has four legs and can't walk?
> A table.

The question suggests some kind of animal, but the answer, following the line of retreat into harmlessness, diverts us from the animal world to the inanimate. If we inquire what line of associations might be thus avoided, we may recall the meaning of various numbers of legs in the riddle of the Sphinx. "Four legs" might then represent a couple in intercourse (cf. Rabelais' "beast with two backs").[38] We could construct here again a latent riddle: Why are a couple in intercourse like a table? Not being able to walk conveys an idea of incapacitation; the excluded onlooker may thus console himself by seeing the united couple as being at a disadvantage.

A great many riddles have to do with sex differences,

particularly those beginning, "What is the difference between——?" For instance:

> What is the difference between a soldier and a lady?
> A soldier faces the powder and a lady powders the face.

While this states a sex difference, it also minimizes it as the soldier and the lady turn out to be surprisingly alike. Many riddles represent the sex difference symbolically and conceal it behind one of less emotional significance. Sometimes no answer is given; the whole aim is to make the one asked feel foolish for not knowing something so obvious.

> "What's the difference between a mail box and a hole in the ground?"
> "I don't know."
> "Then I wouldn't send you to mail letters."

Here the sex difference is expressed partly by a pun (mail—male) and partly by a symbol (hole—female). The person asked is made to undergo something of what the child has suffered when his curiosity and aspirations were frustrated. He is not given any answer and because of his ignorance is excluded from important activities. Riddles in the form of "Why are x and y alike?" are also apt to be concerned with the theme of sex difference; the major effort is then to minimize or deny the difference. In a similar way young children frequently compare those parts of their bodies which are the same for both sexes.

Riddles in the form of "What is it that—?" seem to refer to the sexual organs. There is a series, for instance, about "holes."

> A riddle, a riddle, a hole in the middle. What is it?
> A doughnut.

The puzzling hole is the female genital, for which something harmless is substituted. In another joke about a doughnut, the purchaser pays for it with a nickel which has a hole in it. When the vendor protests, he remarks, "There's a hole in the doughnut too." This expresses the uncertainty whether the hole is something that should be there or not. Other "hole" riddles are:

> What has holes but holds water?
> A sponge.

> What is a lady always looking for but hoping not to find?
> A hole in her stocking.

The first suggests that the female, though she has a hole instead of a penis, is nevertheless able to control her water. The second expresses with slight distortion that a lady is always hoping to find that she has a penis, but finds a hole instead. In another riddle, we are asked how a man who is locked in a church can get out. We are told: "It was a holy church so he got out through the holes." Here we have the question of how the baby gets out of the womb, which is a great puzzle to children before they know about the vagina. This last riddle illustrates a different question form, beginning with "How—". Such questions seem frequently to be about intercourse and birth. In the case of the locked house there are a number of variants having to do with how the man gets in and how he gets out, and which would seem to refer to both the penis and the baby.

Corresponding to the series about "holes," there is a series about the male genital which is represented symbolically as a "key" (an instrument which penetrates a hole). So, for instance,

What's a key that's too big to put in your pocket?
A donkey.

What is the best key to a good dinner?
A turkey.

The first is a fantasy of the huge size of a penis; the second suggests oral incorporation of the desired part. The child's puzzlement about the sexual parts, and difficulty in accepting what he sees, is overtly conveyed in the following spoofing verse recited by an eleven-year-old boy.

> Mommy, Mommy, what is that,
> That hangs on Daddy like a baseball bat?

The mother calls the boy a brat and tells him to ask nursey; nursey, similarly evasive, refers him to his father, who explains:

> Little, little, little brat,
> What hangs on me makes your Mommy fat.

Here the questions and answers, no longer in riddle form, eschew the disguises of the riddles.

Yet another series compares the size of sex organs.

> What president wore the largest hat?
> The one with the largest head.

Here displacement from below to above is used. Related riddles substitute impersonal objects, asking what is the longest pencil in the world, what is the longest word, etc. In these various ways the subjects of the child's sexual investigations, as well as his difficulties in accepting what he finds, are worked over.

Questions of how many seem to refer to the number of siblings. Destructive impulses towards siblings are expressed as there is a tendency to eliminate the total number mentioned. So, for instance:

> There were ten copy-cats in a boat. One jumped out and how many were left?
> None. You see, they were copy-cats, so they all jumped out.

> There were three birds sitting on a fence. A hunter shot one. How many were left?
> None. You see, the others flew away.

In the question of "how many" the child expresses his uncertainty and anxiety about how many more children his parents may have. At the same time, in the instances cited, he expresses his wish to destroy all the siblings.

A riddle on a related theme having to do with numbers states that a mother has nine children and only six apples (or potatoes). How will she divide them evenly? The answer is to make apple sauce (or mashed potatoes). This seems to express resentment against the mother who gives her breast to new babies, while the first child feels there is then not enough food left for him. The fantasy of crushing the apples or mashing the potatoes expresses the cruel wishes of the child towards the mother's breasts which must be shared against his will with the newcomer.

Yet other riddles play with the theme of castration, asking about what sounds like a physical defect. Thus:

> What has eyes but can't see?
> A potato.

> What has ears but can't hear?
> Corn.

A frightening loss of function is suggested, but it turns out not to be what we thought. These riddles are over-determined by the wish to deny impulses to look or listen.

In this sense, it is the good child who has ears but hears nothing, eyes, and sees nothing. Thus again he does not have to fear the punishment which is suggested but warded off.

A perennial joking riddle demonstrates the hazards of knowing by penalizing whoever answers. In the version which I heard in my childhood it went:

> Adam and Eve and Pinch-me went to sea on a raft.
> Adam and Eve fell in and who was left?

The child, if he is sufficiently incautious in his desire to show that he knows, answers, "Pinch-me," and of course receives a sharp pinch. In the version given, the joke refers to the fall of our first parents, which followed from their eating of the tree of knowledge. It conveys the warning: If you think you're so smart, watch out! The one who is eager to show that he knows is punished, just as originally Adam and Eve were punished for gaining forbidden knowledge. We find here the latent rationale of joking riddles and wittily expressed wisdom generally. It is dangerous to know; if one wants to know and yet not be punished, one must at least conceal that one knows.

This joke further expresses a destructive fantasy. How did Adam and Eve happen to fall overboard? We may imagine that it was no accident; they were pushed. Following the Biblical model, Pinch-me is the snake. But perhaps from the child's point of view, Adam and Eve and Pinch-me represent father, mother, and child. It is the violent child who gets rid of the parents by pushing them overboard. The child telling the joke responds to the name of Pinch-me as spoken by the other person, and is summoned to action by it. The name has the property of other jokingly assumed names which we have discussed (My name is Cliff, why don't you drop over some time?)

of serving as a means of attack against the other person. The punishment for the imagined destructive act is diverted from the riddler to his opponent. In the versions of this joke which I have recently heard from children, Adam and Eve are no longer there, but we find instead "Peter and Jack," or "Dickey," or "Nobody." I would guess that the boys' names refer to sibling figures, who have been substituted for the parents as objects of attack. Where we are told "Nobody fell in," the destructive impulse would seem to be further interfered with.

V

A single riddle may sum up the emotional predicament of the child in the wealth of latent content it conceals. The child is represented by his comic counterpart, the moron, whose career we may now proceed to investigate in more detail. Here is one of the moron riddles which I heard most often repeated:

> Why did the moron throw the clock out of the window?
> Because he wanted to see time fly.

Hearing this from one child after another, I was at first baffled at what they could find so interesting in it. We may perhaps begin to understand it if we start with the idea of throwing something out the window. Many children are fascinated by this idea, are strongly tempted to, and frequently do throw various things out of windows. Freud has observed that this act may represent getting rid of unwanted siblings. He was led to this discovery in interpreting a childhood recollection of Goethe's.[39] In his autobiography Goethe recalled that as a young child he threw many pieces of crockery out the window. Freud wondered why this incident was remembered when so much

else was forgotten, and supposed that it must be related
to more important events which were concealed behind it.
He discovered what these events were when he heard from
patients that they had thrown things out the window following the birth of a sibling. The child thus intends in a
magical way to get rid of the unwelcome baby. In Goethe's
case the next children born after him did indeed die. The
memory of throwing things out the window thus symbolized his triumph in getting rid of the unwanted rivals.

Another joke on this theme is explicitly about siblings.
A nine-year-old girl tells: "There were two brothers and
their names were Mike and Mikey. One day their mother
went out shopping and she looked in her purse and saw
she didn't have her key. So she called up and said,
'Michael!'—that was the older brother—'throw out my
key.' So he threw out his brother. You see: my key—
Mikey."

Thus we may suppose that the joke of the moron throwing the clock out of the window conceals the idea of getting rid of an unwanted sibling. But there are also other
components here. The moron "wanted to see" something.
This may refer to the child's overhearing but being unable to see the intercourse of the parents, and reacting
with a raging effort to interrupt it. What the moron
wants to see is something flying, and flying is a symbol
for intercourse. It has been observed that children may
try to interrupt the nocturnal activities of the parents
by wetting and soiling.[40] In fantasies destructive power
is often attributed to defecation.[41] A second meaning of
throwing something out may then be that of excretion.
The joking fantasy of a five-year-old girl which we discussed earlier combines these components of disturbing
the parents at night, uncontrolled defecation, and someone being thrown out the window. In this story, as we may

recall, a cat woke everyone up at night by his loud meow-
ing, defecated continually on people's clothes, and was
thrown out the window by his master. The clock (which
the moron throws out the window) is a symbol of imposed
routines, which in the major early instance are those of
toilet training. Throwing out the clock may thus represent rebellion against the rules of cleanliness. Returning
to the paper of Freud's just cited, we find that the patient
who first provided the clue to the meaning of throwing
things out the window presented together three early
childhood recollections: his father telling him about the
birth of a younger brother, his having thrown things out
the window, and his having shared his parents' bedroom
while on a trip and having made so much noise that his
father beat him. Here we find the twofold connection of
throwing things out the window, with the birth of the
brother, and with disturbing the parents at night.

Ten-year-old Robert, whose mother has recently had a
new baby, has numerous fantasies of throwing things out
the window. He produces what he considers a funny story
about a "mad family." In one episode a new-born baby
knocks a giant out the window. The wish to get rid of the
baby has presumably here given way to the wish to get
rid of the father. The baby becomes the champion who,
on behalf of the boy, performs this feat. In another episode Robert pictures the mother and father fighting each
other with sword and battle axe (sadistic intercourse),
while the son, representing himself, who has been locked
in his room, hits a baseball through the door in the direction of the father. Thus here we find the same combination: the new baby, someone being thrown out the window, and the interruption of the parents in intercourse.
On another occasion Robert talks about disturbing noises
heard at night. He recalls a time when neighbors were

having a very noisy party. He shot his water-gun out the window in the hope of subduing the revellers. He says he wished he had had some stink bombs to throw at them as well. Here the excretory associations of throwing something out the window become explicit.

As the ticking of the clock may symbolize genital pulsations, throwing the clock out may further express the wish to get rid of frightening sexual excitement. The idea of making time fly may have other meanings. The child, envious of the parents, wishes that time would fly so that he could be quickly grown-up and able to do what they do. In this connection throwing something out the window may mean giving birth (which is often symbolized in dreams and fantasies by jumping out of a window). The child wishes that he too could have a baby.

Returning to the manifest construction of the joke, the child uses the expression "time flies" as a sanction for the destructive act of throwing the clock out the window. The children know that, as a seven-year-old girl put it: "There's an expression called 'time flies.' " It is as if the child says, 'You told me time flies,' and takes this as a justification for throwing the clock out the window. We have had occasion to note earlier this tendency of children to twist the adults' words into a sanction of bad behavior. The joke in which the boy misinterprets the mother's request to throw "my key" out the window, and throws out his brother Mikey instead, also illustrates this mocking compliance.

If we are inclined to feel sceptical whether the little joke about the moron throwing the clock out the window can have such a complicated significance, we may recall Freud's observation that jokes, like dreams, are highly condensed. Every detail of the manifest content is apt to be overdetermined by a large number of latent thoughts.[42]

In the present case, each component of the joke—throwing something out the window, wanting to see something, the clock, time flying—stands for much that remains unexpressed. These latent meanings are interrelated in the emotional predicament of the child observing his parents. Their manifest counterparts are connected up in a different way. We are presented with the image of the moron committing a destructive act for what seems like a foolish reason. But the latent content supplies an adequate motivation. The fascination which this joke holds for children derives from the emotional resonance of its hidden meaning. Children of five, as we have seen can express such ideas more openly and fully, as in the joking fantasy of the cat who disturbed everyone at night and got thrown out the window. In the latency period, children come to prefer a more condensed and concealed mode of expression.

The riddle about the moron tiptoeing past the medicine cabinet and the one about throwing the clock out the window present two alternative versions of the child's nocturnal investigations. In the one case, he is pursuing these investigations stealthily and playing dumb to conceal what he has found out. In the other, frustrated at not being able to see, he goes into a destructive rage and disturbs the parents.

The same theme underlies a large number of the moron riddles. The answer to the question of why the moron does something is most often either that he has heard something or that he wants to see something. Some harmless content is regularly substituted for the important object of hearing and seeing. But we may take the clues contained in the verbs, which seem to constitute the less disguised components in the formulation. They suggest the predicament of the curious and frustrated child at night who hears something and would like to see something. The following are instances in which the moron's action is stimulated by his having heard something:

> Why did the moron take a bowl and spoon to the movies?
> Because he heard they had a new serial.

> Why did the moron take the ladder to the party?
> Because he heard the drinks were on the house.

> Why did the moron take the bread and butter to the corner?
> Because he heard there was a traffic jam.

> Why did the moron take his cow to church?
> Because he heard there was a new pastor.

The various situations to which the moron is summoned by having heard something are public performances (movies, church service), dangerous entanglements (traffic jam), or pleasurable and exciting gatherings (party)—which may be taken as symbols of the sexual activities he wants to observe. In each of the instances cited there is an illusory expectation of getting food. What the moron hears fills him with longings, which are expressed in terms of hunger. We may also understand this as a translation of wanting to look, to devour with the eyes, into more primitive oral wishes. Other jokes express the same reversion from looking to eating. The objects to be eaten seem to be either impossible (like the serial) or taboo, as in the following joke told by a seven-year-old girl: "Once a lady went to the movies and she didn't want to pay for her children. So she put them under her pants. Afterwards she asked if they had a good time and they said: 'Yes, we had lemonade and chocolate ice-cream.' You see, she made and they ate it." I would guess there must have

been a version of this joke in which the children got a
"free show." Here, however, forbidden eating is substituted for the forbidden looking. The hunger also represents the feeling of the child who, longing for the mother
at night, experiences a revival of the wish to be fed from
her breast. The long withheld gratification assumes a disgusting aspect, conveying a sour grapes attitude. (We
may recall how the wish for reunion with the mother was
mockingly expressed in the Heinie jokes).

We have already noted several riddles in which the
moron wanted to see something (throwing the clock out
the window to see time fly; putting the television set on
the stove to see Milton Boil). We may add these:

> Why did the moron take the ruler to bed?
> Because he wanted to see how long he slept.
>
> Why did the moron take crayons to bed?
> Because he wanted to see his dreams in technicolor.

Here the nocturnal situation is manifest.

If we consider the most frequent actions of the moron,
to which he is motivated by hearing or wanting to see
something, we find that they are apt to be, on the one
hand, "taking" and, on the other, "throwing" or more
moderately "putting." What he takes may be food, as we
have seen. But also in a number of instances it seems to
be a phallic symbol (he takes a ruler to bed, a gun and
knife to the ball game, a ladder to school or to the party,
etc.). This taking of something phallic would seem to express what the child wants to get from the father, just as
taking food expresses what he wants from the mother.
The child who overhears the parents at night is overcome
by greedy and demanding impulses towards both mother
and father. The throwing and putting (as in throwing
the clock out the window, putting the television set on the

stove) appear to be destructive acts, including execretion as a fantasied means of attack. Thus in the predicament of the moron we find repeated over and over again the situation of the child in his nocturnal isolation, curious, frustrated, longing and enraged. His plight is transformed into a joke by substituting for him the moron who is always doing something ridiculous and who repeatedly demonstrates his incomprehension. The children realize that what the moron is trying to do is impossible, and in laughing at him repudiate their own impossible wishes. We have seen how a similar motive was expressed in the joking fantasies in which five-year-olds represented the fulfilment of their oedipal wishes as absurd. Joking is the opposite of fairy tale wishfulfilment.

VI

Let us now consider the characterization of the joke's protagonist as a moron. We have remarked that the moron represents the opposite of what the latency period child, in his striving for smartness, wants to be. But what is the meaning of the moron's crazy behavior, and how has he become defective? Children, however, enlightened their upbringing, have fears that they may have damaged themselves or made themselves stupid by masturbating. Masturbation itself, with its accompaniment of disturbing fantasies, seems a crazy act. The moron is the child who masturbates. Implicitly that is how he became a moron. Latency period children are involved in an arduous struggle to give up masturbation or to deny their persistence in it. The moron represents what they repudiate in themselves.

It has been observed that children who are undergoing analysis are apt to tell moron jokes at a time when they are approaching, but still evading, the subject of their masturbation.[43] The jokes are a secretive allusion to the forbidden activity. In a similar phase a child may tell about the misbehavior of other children. Speaking of himself in terms of someone else, the child combines confession with denial. It is not he but the moron (or another child) who does such crazy things. We shall see presently how strenuously children attempt to dissociate themselves from the moron.

The moron is frequently pictured as doing odd things in bed. The crayons, ruler, or fishing-rod which he takes to bed with him would seem to symbolize the erect penis. Other things which he takes to bed and which do not belong there, such as oil paints or hay, may refer to soiling or wetting the bed, which are also often expressions of sexual excitement. Sometimes this excitement is expressed in accelerated and inappropriate motor activity. The moron runs around his bed—to catch some sleep. Similarly:

> Why did the moron take the bicycle to bed?
> Because he didn't want to walk in his sleep.

This revolves around the ambiguity of walking: to walk by day, which admits of the preferable alternative of riding, and walking in one's sleep, to which the presumably preferable alternative is lying still. By the pretended confusion of the two kinds of walking, the aim of accelerated motion is substituted for that of reduced activity. This would seem to be in disguised form a story of the child who resolves to renounce masturbation (not to walk) only to resume it more intensively (riding). The nine-year-old girl who told this suffers from sleeping disturbances. She explains the joke by saying: "He's going to ride the bicycle in bed." Thus she takes quite literally the image of nocturnal hyperactivity. We may recall that riding a bicycle is not only a symbol of masturbation, but is frequently used by children as a covert means for performing it.

In the long series of riddles about the moron, he almost always appears alone. He manipulates things, but has no relation to people. We have seen that the latent meaning of the riddles frequently refers to the parents. By presenting on the manifest level the moron alone, the joke isolates the masturbating child from the parents with whom his nocturnal fantasies are occupied. In the child's development conflict about these fantasies is a major factor impelling him to abandon masturbation. The hero of the moron jokes, by his isolation, is able to persist in his crazy behavior of masturbating. The child who feels more constrained can enjoy vicariously the less inhibited behavior of the moron. Masturbation is represented by a variety of motor acts; the moron appears running, riding, climbing, jumping, falling. The structure of the moron riddles resembles that of the riddle of the Sphinx. There also, while the latent content dealt with the parents, on the manifest level there was a single person: man. And he too was represented in motor terms: creeping, walking, hobbling.

The impulsive naughtiness of the moron is not without its perils. Sometimes we see him trying to ward off these dangers, as for instance in the following:

> Why did the moron put hay under his pillow?
> To feed his nightmares.

The punishing beast, who is also a wished-for and feared sexual attacker, is diverted from his prey. We have seen how often the moron is represented as taking something (the mother's breast, the father's penis). Here he is in turn threatened with having something taken from him by a dangerous biting creature. The emphasis on the moron's taking is in part a denial of the danger of his having something taken from him.

Frequently the moron is pictured as venturing recklessly into hazardous situations or as blatantly self-destructive. Thus:

> Why did the moron jump off the Empire State Building?
> Because he wanted to make a smash hit on Broadway.

The huge phallic shape is the father's penis, the sight of which impells the child to competitive exhibition. He hopes to have a sensational success, but also fears a catastrophic defeat. Unable to abandon his ambitions, he pays in advance.[44] The joke presents the sequence: first the suicidal leap, then the theatrical triumph. Fatality is transformed into its opposite. (We may recall how the "bier" became "beer" in a joke we analyzed in the opening chapter.) The Empire State joke presents in a narrow compass the same sequence as that of ancient Greek drama in which the tragedy was followed by the satyr play: after death, triumphant phallic exhibition.

Another self-destructive act of the moron is recorded as follows:

> Why did the moron drive his car over the cliff?
> Because he wanted to test his air brakes.

Is not the silly moron here a lesser Phaeton who wanted like his father to drive a chariot through the air but fell disastrously to earth? The moron impetuously attempts to realize the sexual ambitions from which the child is deterred by his fears. As a six-year-old boy remarks of the moron: "He does things we wouldn't do for anything." The moron, suffering the fate which follows upon his rash

acts, resembles the tragic hero. What is it that makes
him comic instead? Partly it is the abrupt presentation
of the fatal act. This does not give us time to mobilize
sympathetic distress. We have noted this effect before in
connection with exaggerated catastrophes. They strike
us as funny rather than grievous because we are unable
to react adequately to so much disaster so suddenly presented. Since there has been no preparation which would
gradually involve us with the victim and induce us to
suffer empathically, we find ourselves happily detached.
We dispense with the effort to summon up sympathy and
laugh instead. The way in which the motivation of the
protagonist is presented is also important for our reaction. The tragic hero is driven by irrational motives, but
with him we feel the overpowering force of these impulses
more than their irrationality. With the comic hero it is
the reverse. We get an impression of unnecessary foolishness rather than of inevitable drivenness. Almost all the
moron riddles are questions of motive: "Why did the
moron—?" But the manifest act which has been substituted for the underlying desperate desire is an absurd
one. As the boy says: it's something we wouldn't do for
anything. And the reason given is not in terms of urgent
longing, but of an error of thought. The moron is always
making some ludicrous mistake which we can easily see
through. Thus according to Freud's formula of the comic
we laugh at him because he expends less thought than we
would. For children it is less the error of thought than
the exorbitant activity of the moron which they find
funny. This corresponds to the other comic possibility according to Freud: the comic character expends more motor
energy than we would.[45] Since the motor activities of the
moron, as we have seen, may stand for masturbation, his
reckless and incessant movement carries a suggestion of

sexual misbehavior. Such a misbehaving person, if he does not rouse sympathetic alarm, is an object of amusement. Careless of concealment, he offers a pleasurable view of the forbidden.

The self-destructive moron has a pre-history in the funny stories of four- and five-year-old children, who do not yet know the legend of the moron. For four-year-olds a funny or silly character is a legitimate object of wild destruction. But with five-year-olds the plot undergoes a transformation: the silly character damages or destroys himself. In their spontaneous fantasies they have produced an image which will later assume the name and public personality of the moron. Here is a four-year-old boy's idea of a funny story: "A silly old man with a beard—burn him up in the incinerator!" Elated with this fantasy, for which I have given permission by asking him to tell something funny, he dances up and down, pulls my hair and tears up pieces of paper. Other four-year-olds present similar accounts of abrupt and extreme destruction as funny stories. In five-year-olds such joking violence has undergone a marked change. The anticipation of retribution assumes the ascendancy: damage becomes self-damage. Increasing conflict about aggressive impulses occasions the need to disclaim responsibility. The victim is not an object of attack; of his own volition he rushes headlong into catastrophe. He also represents, as we have seen with the moron, the child's sexual impulses through which he fears he has damaged himself. Typical of such joking fantasies of five-year-olds is the one which we discussed earlier about the "silly old man" who loses his teeth, bruises his knee, and pokes holes in his face. In others this silly character precipitates himself into the mouth of a whale, lies in the gutter to get run over, buries himself alive.

A six-year-old boy expresses the feeling that the moron is essentially self-destructive. He has heard the moron jokes from his class-mates, but has not assimilated the stock formulations. He gives rather his own version: "Why did the moron take an axe and buck the window? Because he wanted to cut himself. It makes sense, doesn't it? . . . Why did the moron cut the air to pieces?—Because he didn't want to—because he wanted to be dead, he didn't want to be alive. . . . Why did the moron put his finger in the electricity? Because he wanted to die. . . . Why did the moron lock himself in a drawer?—'Cause he wanted to go to sleep and not have any air for a while." Here the boomerang effects of destructiveness alternate with sheer self-damage.

The moron courts destruction in his general impulsive recklessness. His characterization as a moron indicates that he has already damaged himself. And, as we have seen, he sometimes indulges in grossly self-destructive acts. But he is also an invulnerable hero, surviving each disastrous episode, reappearing ever brash and unchastened. He refuses to learn from the punishment he undergoes, and in his impervious foolishness takes catastrophe for dramatic success.

Before examining the character of the moron further, I should like to consider briefly the theme of "falling" which so frequently in these jokes constitutes the mode of self-destruction and of destruction of objects, and which in general is a perennial gambit of the clown.[46] The emotional significance of falling is complex. Falling originally arouses reactions of fear in infants. But at an early age fear gives way to pleasurable excitement and hilarity. While the fear of the actual fall is thus mastered early and transmuted into fun, the idea of falling retains serious connotations, both sexual and violent. These are reflected in figures of speech. The loss of virtue is a "fall from grace." Adam and Eve "fell," and Lucifer and his cohorts became "fallen angels." Women who have erred are "fallen women." Somewhat less disastrously we "fall in love." Falling is also associated with death and sleep; we "fall asleep," and soldiers "fall" in battle.

Equilibrium sensations are frequently associated with sexual excitement.[47] As the autoeroticism of children is otherwise interfered with, it may become concentrated in motor activities and the accompanying feelings. But the anxiety associated with the sexual excitement is not entirely eliminated. It may develop into neurotic fear of heights, sensations of dizziness, and so on, where the exciting possibilities are almost wholly transformed into anxiety. In common fantasies and dreams we find the double aspect of equilibrium sensations. There are elated dreams of flying and anxiety-ridden ones of falling. As flying frequently symbolizes sexual pleasure, erection or intercourse, falling seems to express feelings of guilt for this pleasure and anticipation of punishment. It may be associated with loss of erection, which is sometimes felt as castration. It also expresses loss of control.

Falling thus combines exciting and anxious feelings. It is peculiarly suited to comic representation because the danger involved may on the manifest level be disposed of as not serious. The physically healthy child, whatever the fate of his sexuality may be, has mastered the problems of equilibrium at an early age. He can walk without falling. It is this counterpoint between manifest mastery and the less controllable hazards of its latent meaning which makes falling the comic act par excellence. While we react on the less conscious level to the latent emotional dangers which the fall expresses, consciously we rest on that triumph of early childhood, having learned to walk. As a child who has achieved this mastery may be observed to laugh hilariously at the tottering of a younger child who is taking his first uncertain steps, so we feel in watching the falls of the comedian that it could not happen to us.

In American film comedies the hero and heroine sometimes fall together, for instance on an icy slope, and this is a symbol and portent of their happy union.[48] But most of the time falling in the literal sense happens to the individual by himself; it is not an interpersonal drama. Thus it is more suited to represent autoeroticism than romance. The clown, the comedian, the moron struggles with the unpredictability and uncontrollability of his own body. In his isolated act of vehement movement and unexpected collapse he does not appear as a possible object of love or a plausible aspirant to it. We have remarked that, in the situation of the moron, the masturbator seems to have been isolated from the personages of the masturbation fantasy. In the manifest joke the moron pursues his absurd activities alone, while the parents, the objects of the masturbation fantasy, are relegated to the latent content. Oedipal fantasies, when separated from the urgencies of autoeroticism so that they can be elaborated at length, become the stuff of serious drama.[49] The substitution of other forms of absurd behavior for the isolated autoerotic act gives rise to a different line of development, that out of which the comedian emerges.

VII

While the moron is a character of recent invention, his prototypes are many and ancient. He is the comic fool of folklore whose absurd behavior and outlandish mistakes embroil him in difficulties and expose him to punishment. Pursuing his impetuous career as an embodiment of unregenerate impulse he is blind to hazards, and miraculously survives them. Often he is not as foolish as he seems. His foolishness is a disguise which insures immunity. As court fool he is permitted to say what is not allowed to others. As servant he outwits and exploits his master. He represents the child in his impulsiveness and irreverence, as well as in the presumed naiveté which grants immunity of expression. He is also an embodiment of the phallus, with its unpredictable ups and downs, its aggressiveness, its susceptibility to dangers, and its fantasied invulnerability.

We have assumed that the moron represents the child, in his nocturnal investigations, frustrations, rages, and autoeroticism. Where we can observe children inventing moron jokes, we see how closely the moron corresponds to themselves. A boy of nearly ten, who is worried that he may be retarded in school, proposes the riddle: "Why is the moron in the first grade when he should be in the tenth?" He goes on to say: "I'm in the fourth grade. I should be in the fifth. All my friends are."

The moron mainly represents an aspect of themselves which children are anxious to repudiate. He is all the things that the latency period child strives not to be: stupid and crazy, reckless and naughty. The child's frustrated longings are translated into the moron's absurdly mistaken expectations (taking a bowl and spoon to the movies because he heard there was a new serial, and so on). In his joking repudiation of his own impossible and forbidden wishes, the child sees the moron as falling into traps which he is much too smart to succumb to. However, the moron is also enviable in his freedom from anxiety, not seeing the hazards he risks. This is expressed in an anonymous bit of American folklore:

> See the happy moron,
> He doesn't give a damn.
> I wish I were a moron—
> My God! perhaps I am.

In the children's conscious feeling, the enviable position of the moron and one's likeness to him are both played down. Children emphatically dissociate themselves from the moron and repudiate his acts. A six-year-old boy says that the moron is someone who "does things we wouldn't do for anything." When asked what, he says that the moron would open his fly and "make a peep." In the course of the conversation the boy has himself behaved in a rather exhibitionistic way, for instance, pulling up his shirt and remarking: "I'm pretty plump." In what he says about the moron he tries to disown his forbidden impulses, as if to say: it is the moron and not I who would do such things.

Children often take the question, "How did the moron get that way?" almost as an accusation. A seven-year-old girl, after having said that the moron is someone who is crazy, replies defensively to the question of how he gets that way: "Don't ask me, ask them." This is as if to say: To know that I'd have to be a moron myself. We may take it as a denial of masturbation; the child claims not to know anything about what makes one a moron. Similarly, a nine-year-old boy says: "I don't know really. It's none of my business. Who wants to be a moron?"

Other children said the moron got that way from not going to school. Since they were in school at the time of being interviewed this would also serve to differentiate the moron from themselves. At the same time it seemed to express a rather disingenuous goody-goody attitude. Others thought the moron's parents had not brought him up right. Thus a seven-year-old boy first laughs at the question of how the moron got that way, says he doesn't know, then: "Maybe he was brought up from the wrong mother and father. They taught him those things. Lots of kids on my block are brought up by the wrong mother and father." Here is again the diversion from the self to other misbehaving children. The thought that it is the fault of the parents is probably a sincere one. Children feel that the parents should guard them against sexual temptations, and on a less conscious level blame the parents for arousing the child's longings. As we have seen from our analysis of the jokes, the moron's crazy behavior is stimulated by what the parents are doing. Other children suppose that the moron was born that way, which may also express an implicit accusation against the parents for having produced a defective child. Yet others say that the moron's head has been hurt or that his brains have worn out. The idea that the moron has become that way from having damaged himself is usually expressed by a reversal: the moron behaves self-destructively because he is a moron. This appears in the manifest content of the jokes where the protagonist is identified as a moron and then described as jumping off the Empire State Building, etc. As the children say: "Who would do things like that except a moron?" Dangerously impulsive behavior is fused with its punishment in the image of the wilfully self-destructive act.

The dissociation of the moron from the child is most strikingly expressed in the fact that most children picture him as a grown man. Asked how old the moron is, a nine-year-old boy says: "I think about forty. You never can really tell. Thirty up to about forty. Maybe twenty. No, not twenty. He looks older. He's tall and skinny. I think he has red hair." A ten-year-old girl remarks, when asked a riddle about the moron going to school:

"That must be the moron's son. A man wouldn't be in school." A ten-year-old boy, asked how old the moron is, says: "Probably a good forty or fifty years old." "Could he be a child?" "I don't think they'd say that about a child. They'd say 'the crazy child' and not 'the moron.' " An eleven-year-old girl says that she used to picture the moron as "a tall, thin man. There're a lot of jokes about the 'little moron,' I never pictured him. But a tall man in blue, brown,—no, grey trousers, a blue shirt, yellowy brown hair, like you see in pictures but not really, long Scandinavian hair, running as fast as he could, leaping past a wall with an advertisement for food. I don't know what riddle that comes from. Maybe the one about the pastor."

In the moron jokes current among adults the stock term is "the little moron." [50] The children I talked with regularly dropped the "little." However, on occasion they demonstrated that the retention of this adjective would not have precluded the moron's being a grown man. After all we have the expression "a little old man." In keeping with this, a thirteen-year-old girl describes the moron as "a little old guy, with his hair in little tails, a black suit, and a purple tie. A regular jerk." Sometimes the moron is represented as fantastically old. An eleven-year-old boy says: "His brain must have worn out. Lets make him two-thousand years old. I think his brain would wear out by then." A nine-year-old boy seems to be under the impression that a moron is a pre-historic creature: "Something that isn't living. Some kind of animal that isn't living." Asked on another occasion about the moron, he pictures him as "a cuckoo-looking drunk." "How old is he?" "Two-hundred-and-fifty years."

Thus the moron, the representative of the child, is disguised as a man, an old, even a fantastically old, man. We

may guess that the father has here been substituted for
the child. The motives for this substitution are complex.
We may recall how four- and five-year-old children produced original funny stories about silly old men and silly
old women. At four, these silly old people were apt to be
targets for abrupt violence. At five, they became self-
destructive, pulled out their teeth, poked holes in their
faces, and so on. The child defends himself against the
expected boomeranging of his destructiveness by a projection onto the parents. From being the victims of his
rage, they become, as his anticipation of retribution increases, the bearers of his self-destructiveness—at least in
his joking fantasies. There is an aspect of the parents'
behavior which further facilitates the projection of the
moron image, namely their crazy nocturnal violence.
Thus it is not the moron-child-masturbator who is crazy,
but the parents in the sexual act who are much more so.
Again we see the relation of joking to the degradation of
parental authority, as the sexual side of the parents occasions disillusionment and mockery.

We have still to explain why the moron is a man rather
than a woman. But then most clowns and comic characters
are male. Why this should be so is a complicated question,
to which I shall suggest only some tentative answers.
What is funny about the woman is that she lacks an ana-
tomical part. But both sexes seem to find it difficult to
consider this funny. The fear of the male and the chagrin
of the female which are aroused by this fact seem difficult
to transmute into a joke. What we often find instead is
the compensatory idealization of the female figure, notably in painting and sculpture. What is funny in the
man is the unpredictable behavior of the penis. This is
functional rather than structural, and so readily trans-
latable into comic action. Thus we get the characteristic

gambits of the clown or comedian with his unexpected
movements, his alternate collapses and surprising hyperactivity. Action is more susceptible to comic elaboration
than structure. Absurd behavior has a greater comic impact than plastic distortions. Moreover, according to
Freud, distortions of shape gain their comic effect by
producing an illusion of absurd movements.[51] An exaggeratedly large nose, for instance, gives the impression
of a nose being extended; it follows the model of phallic
activity. Also it is mainly men who produce works of art,
including the comic; and they apparently find it easier
to transform jokingly aspects of their own sexuality
rather than that of the woman which remains strange and
uncanny to them. A further factor would seem to be that
the contrast between the role of authority and the sexual
role is more pronounced in the father than in the mother.
The child has had access to the mother's body in a way
which presages later sexual intimacies. The father is more
remote and alien to such feelings and fantasies. He appears more purely grand, important, knowing, and law-
giving. His crazy nocturnal sexuality thus appears more
incongruous, suggesting comic possibilities.

The association of the moron with the father appears
in an original riddle of a nine-year-old boy: "Why does
the moron go to school when he knows everything? I don't
know the foolish answer to that. Maybe because he likes
it." This boy's father was still in college during the boy's
early childhood. The father's studies kept him often occupied and imposed constraint and quiet on the child. The
boy later manifested learning difficulties, which the mother
attributed to his resentment of the father's studies and to
the impression that learning must be something exces-
sively difficult since the father was still working at it. In
the riddle to which he cannot find the answer the boy ex-

presses his puzzlement about the father: Does he know everything or doesn't he? Isn't he a moron to be still in school though he's a grown-up man and a father? The boy follows this with a riddle referring to himself which I mentioned before: "Why is the moron in the first grade when he should be in the tenth? . . . I'm in the fourth grade. I should be in the fifth." Thus he is retarded in school just as his father seemed to be, the defective son of a defective father. With the intensity of personal meaning of the moron for him, it is not surprising that he shows a particularly strong need to make the moron something remote. It is he who conceives of a moron as a prehistoric animal.

VIII

Let us now view the joking of latency period children in a developmental perspective. The preferred joke forms of these children contrast with those both of younger children and of adolescents. We have seen that latency period children have a great liking for jokes expressed in a concise verbal formula, like the riddle, which they can learn and repeat exactly. Beneath this verbal formula is a latent meaning which has been drastically condensed and disguised. The child values the joke's concealment of material which he is anxious to repress. He also strenuously denies that the joke has any relation to himself. This appears particularly in his dissociation of himself from the joke's protagonist, the moron.

These qualities of the learned formula, with its conciseness, precision, and concealment, so valued by the latency period child, seem to have little appeal for children under six. They do not learn ready-made jokes, but rather tell funny stories of their own invention. While these may deal with the same themes as the joking riddle, the form is quite different. It tends to be a rambling narration rather than a finished verbal formula. The child lets his thoughts go and welcomes whatever absurdity may occur to him. Having access to these inner resources the young child does not seem to need the ready-made joke. Children of four and five do not pick up the joking riddles from older brothers or sisters or friends, or from slightly older children with whom they are in constant contact. In a school play-yard, where five-year-old children mingled daily with children just turned six, I found that the older ones knew a stock of joking riddles, but the younger ones had not picked them up.

When I tried to teach joking riddles to five-year-old children, they seemed to find them meaningless. I asked Nora, the five-year-old girl who had made up the funny story about the cat that got thrown out the window: "Do you know why the moron threw the butter out the window?" As she said she didn't know, I told her: "To see the butterfly." She smiled slightly but, I felt, without comprehension. I explained that it was a joke. Nora said: "My brother knows those but I don't." (Nora's brother is eleven.) When I asked if she knew any other jokes like that, she said: "I'll show you on a piece of paper." She proceeded to draw and told me: "See, a man got so funny he fell in the water and a whale swallowed him. . . . Here's the man and here's the whale." Pointing to the whale: "Here's eyes and two noses. No, here's an eye and a nose and an eye and a nose. No, one eye." She laughed. Thus she reverts to her own style of original joking fantasy. She has her own counterpart to the moron in her funny man who plunges so abruptly into catastrophe. And she plays with the idea of losing and gaining body parts (the varying numbers of eyes and noses) more freely than we would find it in the riddles.

The imperviousness of the child under six to the joking riddles appears in an intelligent four-year-old girl whose constant playmate was a neighbor girl of seven. On a visit to the younger child's house, I asked her if she could tell me any jokes or funny stories. The older girl, who happened to be there, immediately volunteered: "Why did the moron sleep in the fireplace?—Because he wanted to sleep like a log." And so on through a considerable repertoire. Ignoring this recital, the four-year-old furrowed her brow, thinking up her own funny story. Finally she came out with a rambling account of how a tree was broken by a storm, people glued it together, but it was broken again by the rain, and so on. This is again a fantasy of violent damage (here expressed symbolically in terms of impersonal objects) such as four-year-olds characteristically consider funny.

If one can persuade a five-year-old child to pay attention to a riddle, one sees him reacting in his own way, incorporating it into his fantasy life. Where the latency period child who learns a new riddle commits it to memory with the idea of telling it to his friend, the younger child ignores the clear sharp form and allows its meaning to merge with his other thoughts. Five-year-old Ann (whose funny stories about the silly old man and silly old woman we have discussed before) assimilated a joking riddle I told her in this way. We were in the play-yard shared by the fives and young sixes and I had been trying to get Ann's reaction to "Why did the moron throw the butter out the window?" Some six-year-old girls joined us, asked what we were talking about, and volunteered other riddles. Ann then said she wanted to tell me a story. It was about a family of bears. The father bear has eaten a hoot owl. The little bears do not understand what has happened and question the mother. She explains that father did it because he was so hungry. Then a lion appears and asks: "Where's the female?" Ann explained that "female" means "girl." She interrupted her story to ask about the necklace I was wearing: was it a double string of pearls, and had I ever seen a quadruple string. Then she wanted to know: what do you call six babies that are all born from the same seed? At this point she wanted to make a "joke part" to her story. As I was about to write this on a separate page, she indicated that she meant it to be continuous with what had gone before. She tried to recall: "What was that? Why did something throw the butter out the window?" One of the six-year-old girls supplied the word "moron." Ann continued: "Why did the moron throw the butter out the window? Because the bear told him to and the lion told him to. The bear and the lion were silly. That's why they told the moron to throw the butter out the window."

Ann's story, so full of sexual questionings, was probably stimulated by the previous exchange of riddles. She seems to have responded to the latent meaning of the moron's throwing something out the window, the child's rage at the parents' nocturnal activities and wish to get rid of the babies they produce. In her fantasy of ravenous father bears and lions who demand "Where's the female?" she makes explicit what the riddle conceals. And she makes this "silliness" of the parent-figures the provocation for the moron's violence. In so doing she dissolves the riddle form, with its isolation of the moron's act, and weaves the riddle into the context of her fantasy.

The preference for a concise joke form only begins with latency. It is the special requirements of this age which give rise to the style of joke based on verbal economy and an abrupt conclusion. These stylistic devices remain as a permanent acquisition; they are the distinctive contributions of the latency period to the realm of wit. Freud has discussed the function of brevity in wit and its relation to surprise. The release afforded by the joke must be sufficiently sudden so that the freed energy may not be assimilated into other channels but is discharged in laughter.[52] However, a five-year-old child rhapsodically improvising a joking fantasy may produce many surprise effects in the course of an interminable narration. The child allows his spontaneous thoughts to come to the surface and does not know what is coming next. He has been invited to think of something funny, and so in the course of telling he has his characters suddenly go naked or perform other wild acts, which evoke laughter from himself and other children. The requirement for conciseness in the preferred jokes of latency period children expresses interference with this free flow of fantasy. With the onset of latency much of the earlier fantasy activity is repressed. We have seen how these repressed fantasies constitute the latent content of the joking riddles, and that in the formation of the joke they have undergone a process of compression and substitution. The concise joke comes to an abrupt and decisive end, which precludes thinking or inquiring any further. This joke convention expresses the renunciation of the free and endless flow of fantasy of the earlier period.

The fact that latency period children learn rather than invent their jokes is related to the same inhibition of fantasy. The ready-made joke has a social sanction which individual improvisation lacks. The conventional joke form has a similar virtue. Thus latency period children, in the jokes they invent, often attempt to conform to the convention of the joking riddle. They model their own jokes on others which they have learned. The guilt which has overtaken their private fantasies is reduced by the adoption of shared modes of expression.

The latency period child also exhibits a motor restraint while telling jokes which contrasts with the behavior of younger children. A five-year-old child, asked to tell something funny, begins at once to smile, giggle, teeter, and topple. Telling something funny at this age is intimately related to acting funny. The verbally funny has not been isolated from comic behavior. Latency period children tend much more to recite their repertoire of joking riddles in a spirit of displaying items of learning. What is funny has become concentrated in the verbal formula, which is now separable from a comic performance. It is the moron in the joke and not the child telling it who behaves in a ridiculous way. The latency period joke teller, with his learned jokes, does not abandon himself to the spontaneity either of fantasy or of movement. While clowning and horseplay are of course common in latency period children, their verbal joke telling tends to be more isolated from comic behavior than is the case with either younger or older children.

The telling of a joke in which an exact verbal formula is to be reproduced, as in the joking riddles, neither requires nor allows for any artistry in the telling. If one knows the correct wording that is all that is necessary. One of the striking changes in the attitude towards joke telling that occurs as children grow out of latency is that this sheer verbal reproduction ceases to be satisfying. Increasingly from about eleven or twelve on, children tell jokes in anecdotal form, in which the telling is not a verbatim repetition but leaves something to the ingenuity of the teller. How the joke is told, wording, timing, mimicry become increasingly important. In adolescence children talk about the skills required for telling certain kinds of jokes. They will say, for instance, that someone else can tell certain jokes which they cannot because you have to imitate certain accents. Thus for adolescents (or even in some cases starting with prepuberty) joke telling becomes an art. What should we call the joke telling of the latency period by contrast? It would seem to be more like a science than an art, since it depends entirely on knowing something, knowing the correct words, knowing the answer to the riddle. However, since what is known is purely verbal, and as we have seen empirical investigation is strenuously denied, we should perhaps draw an analogy to ritual rather than to science. The joking riddles resemble rituals in that they require the exact repetition of a verbal formula. There is also a resemblance to ritual in the prominence of defense against dangerous thoughts, in the tendency to keep the latent meaning quite far below the surface. With adolescence these jokes become too mild, and tend to be replaced by the sort which, after concealing a sexual or destructive idea, then brings it out.

As joke telling becomes an art the verbal recital becomes fused with comic performance. The joke teller mimics the protagonists of his anecdote. Thus the combination which we noted in younger children, who accompanied the telling of funny stories with comic behavior, is revived on a higher level. Following the isolation of the verbal joke from comic acting in latency, the two components tend to merge again. There has been, however, a considerable transformation. Where the younger child's acting funny while telling something funny is an expression of his own excitement and voluntary abandonment of control, for the older joke teller the comic performance illuminates the content of the joke. Where the younger child's acting funny is mainly motor, the older joke teller's comic performance is largely conveyed in tones of voice. In the telling of a joking riddle, the tone of voice is irrelevant. It is only a question of getting the words right. The preferred jokes of the latency period children thus require no mimicry. But this is again related to something else which we have observed, namely the children's strenuous efforts to dissociate themselves from the protagonist of the joke, the moron.

In adolescence the need to dissociate oneself from the comic protagonist becomes much less intense. There is an increased tendency to impersonate the characters in the joke. This becomes possible as the dialogue form replaces the riddle. While latency period children also tell some jokes in dialogue form, such jokes are less frequent with them, and the words spoken rather than the manner of speaking tend to be exclusively important. The fear of assuming the moron's role, which we have observed in latency period children, is reduced in adolescents. They are more inclined, for instance, to mimic the moron. A thirteen-year-old girl says: "He's a guy who looks like this," and puts on a blank expression, letting her tongue hang out. Where a latency period child is apt to assure us in a somewhat apprehensive way that no one in his school is a moron, adolescents may remark jokingly that many of their classmates are morons. Or an adolescent may suggest teasingly that a friend who is present is a moron (this all being provoked by a discussion of moron jokes and the question of what is a moron). Having thrown out a mocking hint to this effect about her friend, a twelve-year-old girl says: "It's not necessarily like you —it could be like me." We have come a long way from the latency period child who had to define the moron as a prehistoric animal to insure its remoteness from himself.

Adolescents sometimes explicitly prefer jokes where the protagonists resemble themselves. They may for this reason repudiate the moron jokes, not because of the foolishness of the moron, but because they find his behavior too far-fetched, or as they put it, "unrealistic." The remoteness from the self which was of such value to latency period children becomes negative. A thirteen-year-old girl with whom I have been discussing the moron jokes, which she no longer likes, tells one of the sort she now prefers. A woman goes into the butcher shop and says: "I want a pound of kidleys." The butcher says: "You want a pound of kidneys?" And the woman says: "That's what I said, did'll I?" The girl remarks: "That's a little more realistic. The same thing happened to me. I was going to get some blintzes and I asked for 'plintzes.' Jokes like that seem real. They're cute. You'll laugh when you make your own mistake yourself."

Another requirement for joke telling which becomes prominent as children emerge from latency is the presence of the appropriate mood. While latency period children frequently speak of their "hilarious" moods and the uncontrollable laughing fits that they get into with their friends, they do not say that they would have to be in the mood to tell jokes. Their joke repertoire can be readily produced upon request. With children of eleven and twelve, one gets repeatedly the protest that they cannot tell jokes just "cold," that they have to be in the mood, that the occasion has to be auspicious. Thus with them, as with the younger (pre-latency) children, joke telling involves an abandonment of restraint, contact with the inner sources of spontaneity. However, while with the younger children the permission of the adult is an adequate condition for inducing this mood, with the older children it is no longer so. They find it difficult to think of, or tell jokes when asked by an adult. Closely related to the requirement of mood and atmosphere is the demand

that the joke should be relevant to the situation in which
it is produced. This is also increasingly specified by prepuberty and adolescent children.

In adolescent joke telling we thus see an increased infusion of comic acting, a readier recognition of kinship
with the joke protagonists, and an increased requirement
of relevance to mood and situation. As we see how all these
aspects contrast with latency period joke telling, we are
struck with the extent to which the latter is dominated by
the mechanism of isolation. The preferred latency period
joke, such as the joking riddle, is isolated from comic performance, the protagonist is dissociated from the self, and
the relation of the joke to mood and situation is minimal.
In all this we see the height of the defences which latency
period children erect around the impulses which the jokes
express.

IX

We have remarked how sexual curiosity provides the
motive of the joking riddles. I should now like to trace the
earlier and later forms of joking which express the same
theme. In four- and five-year-old children a favorite form
of joking begins: "Did you ever hear of—" or "Whoever
heard of—." This is followed by something which the
child considers absurd. For instance, at a lunch which included meat-loaf and beets, a four-year-old boy asked
jokingly: "Did you ever hear of a beet-loaf?" This led
to a series of similar questions which other children joined
in propounding. The unheard-of things included danger
situations ("Did you ever hear of a ferryboat that went
under water?"), the slightly taboo ("Did you ever hear
of a toilet in the bath-tub?" "Did you ever hear of
Shut-up?"), and nonsensical phrases ("Did you ever
hear of a house house?"). A five-year-old girl produces a

long series of such joking questions, among them: "Whoever heard of someone up in the sky, walking up in the sky? . . . Whoever heard of someone who was going away, and they went zip right away like zipper? . . . Whoever heard of someone painting a picture and the window was closed and the picture flew right out the window when there was no window open? . . . Whoever heard of a plant that was growing and it was an orange seed and when it was growing apples came out of it? . . . Whoever heard of someone who was turning out the light and when they turned out the light it wouldn't go out? . . . Whoever heard of somebody who was walking on the sidewalk and whoever they bumped into they went right through them, it was just like air?" The sexual reference of some of these questions is fairly patent, as in the last one dealing with the mystery of how one body can penetrate another, or the one about the queer development of seeds. Others in more disguised form anticipate the joking riddles, using the symbolism of flying, closed windows, and so on.

What is the difference between these joking questions and the riddles? The joking questions do not require an answer. Rather the answer is understood: no one ever heard of such outlandish things. We may take this as a denial: the objects of the child's sexual investigations do not exist. Their queerness (represented in terms of substitute objects) is exaggerated to the point where no one could believe in such a thing. At the same time there is a denial that the child heard (of) anything at night. But there is at the same time an affirmation: what has been heard (of) is something very crazy. To the child's way of feeling the nocturnal behavior of the parents is quite mad. The joking question carries the force of an amazed and condemnatory exclamation: Whoever heard of such a thing!

How is this changed in the joking riddle? The riddle must be answered. The issue of knowing or not knowing becomes central. The child re-enacts in a parodied way the course of his own frustrated investigations and assuages his hurt vanity by putting someone else in the position of not knowing the answer. All the old questions are repeated ("What is the difference between—?" "What is it that—?" "How does he get out?" etc.) in what seems like a parody of the endless uncertainties of the obsessive neurotic. In the moron riddles, as we have seen, it is the child himself who becomes the central protagonist; it is his sexual craziness rather than that of the parents which constitutes the plot. But why does the moron do such crazy things, why does he rage, destructive and self-destroying? Because he has heard something, or because he wants to see something. Thus we found the allusion to the parents' sexual activity in the latent content of the joke. But it was the child's reactions to his investigations and the child's autoerotic activity which provided the model for the manifest plot, in which the moron performs his solitary foolishness.

In pre-puberty and early adolescence we find again joking questions which do not require an answer. Children who are getting bored with riddles often ask questions like the following: "Did you ever see a horse fly?" "Did you ever see a cat fish?" "Did you ever see a honey bear?" The hearer, if he gets the point, realizes that no answer is required. These recall the joking questions of four- and five-year-old children, though we see that there are obvious differences. The joking questions of the older children involve a double meaning. Let us examine the two meanings in "Did you ever see a horse fly?" The first is that of a flying horse. This would be just the sort of thing we would find in the joking questions of the younger children, something amazing and improbable. But with the second meaning, that of the horsefly, we are brought down to earth. Something commonplace, trivial and even slightly disgusting is substituted for the marvellous and incredible. Yes, we have seen a horsefly. In other words, the object of earlier curiosity is now drastically devalued. Earlier dreams and fantasies are being deflated. The final conflict with, and effort to repudiate the Oedipus complex is being inaugurated. Jokingly the children say in effect: What were we so excited about? If the flying horse-into-horsefly represents the father's penis which does not seem so overwhelmingly big any more, the fishing cat represents the dangerous female genital. By the word play this threat also disappears. Instead of the cat who will catch and consume the fish, we find the catfish secure by himself. The honey bear (honey bare) also represents the dissolution of a danger. The dangerous beast (father-figure) disappears, and we find instead the desired woman.

The joking question which for younger children was an exclamation of amazement becomes for the older children just the opposite. It conveys a blasé attitude: there's nothing to get excited about. The competition in knowing, which was so important in the riddles, disappears. The joking question requires no answer. Laughing together, the teller and hearer imply that they know all about it and need say no more. For a moment the hearer may think he is being asked a riddle, until he sees that the question answers itself. He is first impelled to deny that he has seen what the question asks about, but then he realizes that he has seen it after all. Thus the denial of having seen is finally abandoned. The reduction of the importance or dangerousness of the thing seen makes this possible. There is a component of comic acting on the side of the one who asks the question, as he must create a momentary illusion that he expects an answer. There is much more an atmosphere of comedy about these questions than about the latency period riddles. This is in keeping with the underlying thought: don't take it seriously. I should add that these joking questions are not as numerous or as frequently told as the joking riddles of the preceding phase. They are significant, however, as a gesture of farewell to the riddles.

The dramatization of a blasé attitude occurs in another kind of joke which is popular with adolescents. This is what is known as the "shaggy dog story." The formula of this type of joke is that something very far-fetched happens and that someone grossly underreacts to it. For instance, a man is playing chess with a dog. An onlooker, after observing the performance for some time, exclaims that it is the most remarkable thing he ever saw. The owner of the dog says: "Oh, he isn't so good. I've beaten him one game out of three." We can see in this type of joke another variant on the theme of remarkable things seen and heard. It is more complicated than the flying horse-into-horsefly joke though it expresses a similar devaluation. In the shaggy dog story we have a comic drama in which one of the protagonists gives us the cue for reducing our amazement by his lack of response. In the instance given, the man who reacts so slightly commits a comic error of thought. By a displacement of emphasis he mistakes the bystander's remark to mean not that it is a marvel that a dog plays chess, but that the dog is the best chess player he has ever seen. He corrects this by pointing out that the dog is not unbeatable. As a result of the displacement an explanation is avoided; we are never told how it is that the dog can play chess. The story has led us to expect an explanation of a highly improbable event, but instead we are told in effect that the event is nothing to get excited about. At this whatever effort we have been making to suspend disbelief collapses. The remarkable event is laughed off as sheer nonsense. The essential cue is provided by the protagonist who regards the amazing as commonplace and as requiring no explanation. The animals who behave like human beings in these jokes may be interpreted in the reverse sense as representing human beings who behave like animals. Thus we are brought back to the initial occasion of the child's amazement, the sexual behavior of the adults. The shaggy dog story, though by different means, combines the effects of the younger and older children's joking questions. We are shown that an amazing event can be taken entirely casually, and besides we realize it never happened.

Here is a joke of this type which leads up to a joking question. It was told by a sixteen-year-old boy. "A man left a million dollars to his son on condition that he keep a fur coat intact for ten years. The coat has a million hairs and he counts them every year. You go through each year and he counts them over at great length. Finally at the end of the tenth year there's one hair missing. And he sees a little moth flying around and he says: 'Did you eat that hair?' and the moth says: 'Yes.' And he says: 'I'm going to squash you and get that hair.'—Did you ever hear a moth bawl?"

In this joke we find a boy being warned by his father that he will suffer a grievous loss if he fails to keep a valuable object intact. We can readily translate this into its underlying meaning: a threat of castration in connection with masturbation. The valuable object which must be guarded is really the same as that which is in danger of being lost; both are referred to by a "million" (dollars, hairs). The warning against masturbation produces the opposite of the intended effect. The boy, in constant anx-

iety about the intactness of the valuable object, must reassure himself by continually manipulating it (counting
the million hairs—masturbating a million times). The
moth represents the father, greatly diminished (cf. flying
horse-into-horsefly). The castrative damage which he effects is similarly represented as minute (eating a single
hair). The story attempts to protect the boy against loss
by multiplying the valuable part by a million, but the
defense is imperfect. The disappearance of one out of a
million counts as a total loss (he will lose the million—
dollars). However, the boy has now grown very big, and,
following a frequent line of fantasy, the father has in the
meanwhile grown very small. The boy can easily crush the
father. In the effort to reduce the oedipal emotions this
crime becomes a very trivial act, the squashing of an in-
sect. Despite its triviality, the act remains an all-impor-
tant one for the hero of the joke, and this disproportion
contributes to the comic effect.

How shall we interpret the question: "Did you ever
hear a moth bawl?" In form it resembles other joking
questions which begin with "Did you ever hear—" and
may be taken as referring to what the child hears at
night. The intercourse of the parents is here condensed
with the father-killing to which the son feels motivated
by it. What about the double meaning of "moth bawl?"
Moth balls protect your clothes, and clothes protect your
balls; or, in the symbolism of the joke, the coat itself
stands for the genitals. Thus the thought of defense
against castration is again expressed. Killing the father
(making the moth bawl) is the best protection (moth
ball). At the beginning of the story the father has already
died, we do not know how. That the son feels guilty is
shown by his anxiety about the intactness of his valuable
possession. His murderous impulses towards the father

come out at the end, directed towards the diminished father-surrogate, the moth.

The theme of inheritance from the father has yet another meaning; the father's death is a means to securing the mother. The million dollars which the son hopes to get and is so uncertain of getting thus refers to what was first the father's and what the son intensely covets: the mother. The joke breaks off without telling us whether the son gets the inheritance or not. But it is just through this device that it achieves its most important effect. The impact of the joke depends on our having been concerned however slightly with whether the boy gets his inheritance. When the narration breaks off with the foolish question: "Did you ever hear a moth bawl?" our involvement with the imaginary situation dissolves. We cease to care whether the boy gets the inheritance or not. Or rather the situation becomes to us totally unreal. In jokes and stories generally there are many degrees of implausibility, and our willing suspension of disbelief and sympathetic involvement with imaginary characters admits correspondingly of many degrees. The situation in this joke, despite its initial implausibility, involves our interest because of the underlying meaning. But having been drawn into this imaginary predicament, as it were against our better judgment, we suddenly realize at the end that the whole issue of the great inheritance is an unreal one, and we stop caring about it. Thus the emotional drama of the joke consists in a reenactment of oedipal renunciation. The solution is not one of getting the inheritance or losing it but of ceasing to care about it. While in its manifest plot the joke breaks off without reaching a solution, in its emotional sequence a solution is reached. This is the significance of all the jokes of this type, in which some expected explanation or event fails to materialize in the manifest story. The process involved is one in which we reenact the lessening of our concern with childhood questions and wishes.

In its formal structure the "moth bawl" joke resembles the five-year-old's treatment of the riddle, namely by giving it a setting in a rambling story. Here as in several other respects adolescent joke telling revives characteristics of pre-latency. The tight concise form preferred by latency-period children gives way to more free-flowing narration. The narrator must be skillful and becomes to some extent a comic performer, particularly in the rendering of dialogue. The boy who told the "moth bawl" joke, for instance, assumed a grimly determined tone while impersonating the son and gave the moth a high squeeky voice. Thus he brought out the reversal of parent and child roles, and also probably imputed castratedness to the moth (father) by the high-pitched voice. Adolescent boys frequently find such high voices (in other jokes explicitly those of male figures) very funny, presumably because of the implied sissy (castrated) character.

Such jokes contrast in another way with those preferred by latency-period children, namely in the risk which the teller incurs. In the joking riddle the risk is on the side of the hearer, whose ignorance is exposed, or who may be penalized for answering (as, for instance, in the Pinch-me riddle). With the "moth bawl" and similar jokes, the risk is on the side of the teller. He must by his skill ward off a too early protest by the hearer that the whole thing is ridiculous. It is he rather than the hearer who is apt to look foolish. In telling his absurd story he is departing from the realm of reasonable discourse, and to succeed he must be able to carry his hearer with him. The boy who told the "moth bawl" joke remarked that you "have to feel silly" to tell jokes like that. This silliness would seem to mean partly a feeling of accessibility of irrational thinking, partly a readiness to assume a comic role. We have noted the frequently expressed requirement of adolescents that for joke telling there must be a proper mood. The teller must feel ready to say something which at other times would sound too foolish and the hearers must be ready to go along with him.

<h2 style="text-align:center">X</h2>

All the jokes which we have discussed (I speak now of the ready-made jokes and not the improvised funny stories of the four- and five-year-olds) may of course be told by adults, as they also no doubt originated with adults. Efforts of latency-period children to invent joking riddles regularly fall short of the formal requirements exemplified, for instance, in the moron series. While the original jokes which children make are not adequate to adult standards, and are likely to impress adults as funny mainly by their ineptitude, the fact remains that there is a wide range of overlap in the jokes told by children and adults. In adult joke telling there is a readiness for regression which may under the proper conditions reach to any level of infantility. Also among adults there are wide differences in education and taste which affect joke preferences. The main point about the relation of joke preferences to different age levels would seem to be this. Jokes represent a certain way of overcoming emotional difficulties. They vary in content and in form depending on the phase of development whose characteristic impulses and defenses they express. The preference of children of a certain age for a certain kind of joke gives us a clue to its underlying significance, which may be further confirmed by the analysis of the joke itself. Thus the joking riddles and the moron jokes appeared both in terms of the children's preferences and on the basis of an analysis of their content to be peculiarly related to the problems of the latency period. They are the comic accompaniment of the child's serious preoccupation with learning during this time and express his mixed feelings about knowledge. Sexual questionings are pursued in a disguised form, and the inadequate answers of the parents as well as the incomplete understanding of the child are parodied. The desperate concern with being smart is partly gratified and partly mitigated in the joking riddle. It is the hearer who cannot answer, and the moron in the joke, not the child who tells it who is stupid. The vicissitudes of autoeroticism are displaced onto the moron who is sharply dissociated from the self. As we have seen all these tendencies become reduced in prepuberty and adolescence; the joking riddles and moron jokes are apt to be devalued. However, the emotional difficulties of each phase of life continue to be to some extent unfinished business. We never graduate from them as decisively as we do from school grades. Thus we may continue to enjoy jokes whose emotional sources are in various past stages of development.

The repudiation of joking riddles and moron jokes in prepuberty and early adolescence has a sharpness which seems to express the contempt children have for the childishness of their own recent past. In later adolescence children say they sometimes enjoy "resuscitating all those bad jokes" (as a sixteen-year-old boy put it) when they are being intentionally silly. That is, telling them takes on a comic quality: I'm playing the fool in telling this. Some time in adulthood one abandons the sense of age-grading, of pride in differentiating oneself from a younger group. Then, among other things, the range of jokes from different ages becomes more readily accessible.

CHAPTER 4

Development
of the Joke Façade

I

JOKES are a way of enjoying something otherwise forbidden. As we grow up we become aware of restrictions which others impose on our sexual and hostile impulses, and develop inner restraints. Joking is a means of circumventing these inhibitions in ourselves and disarming others. The joke construction makes it possible for us to satisfy sexual or hostile impulses and yet be free of conscious shame or guilt. Thus there is a double aspect to the joke: the sexual or hostile theme and the joke façade which gets it past inner and outer censorship.[53] The need for the joke façade develops gradually in children as their awareness of outer restrictions and their inhibitions increase with age. In the present chapter I shall trace the stages of this development.

Let us first observe how the joke façade functions in an adult joke. A British anthropologist was visiting an isolated African tribe. There he was told: "You know, we follow British legal procedure here. We know all about it from reports we've read of British trials." When he was taken to witness a trial, he was amazed to see how exactly the forms of a British court had been reproduced. Counsels in wigs disputed the case with great punctilio. There was just one thing that puzzled him. Every now and then a man ran through the assembled crowd and touched all the women's breasts. Finally he asked his informant about this. The man told him: "We always read in the accounts of your trials, 'A titter ran through the audience.' "

This anecdote evokes an image of sexual freedom in the fortunate man who can touch all the women's breasts. But this fantasy in itself would not be entirely gratifying; we would be too aware of the obstacles which make such conduct impossible for us. Since the action takes place in a "primitive" tribe, we might anticipate that greater freedom prevails there. But then we are told that they accept our laws with all their constraints. The problem thus arises how is such sexual freedom compatible with these laws? The line "A titter ran through the audience" gives the solution. The phrase, taken as a prescription of decorum, is interpreted in such a way as to permit and even require the forbidden sexual pleasure. The wit technique involves a comic error of thought, a misunderstanding made possible by verbal ambiguity. (The construction is the same as in the moron jokes where an absurd act follows from the misunderstanding of an ambiguous word. Only here the action is more gratifying to adults than the mad behavior of the moron.) The word play and the comic mistake, which are in themselves harmlessly amusing, divert our attention from the sexual content which we can thus enjoy as it were incidentally. The discovery of a phrase which can be understood as both respectable and indecent makes it possible to express rebellion against forbidding authorities by a mocking compliance. The African tribesmen of the story appear foolish in their misunderstanding, but they have found a clever way of circumventing the law to which we remain subjected.

In the jokes which children tell at different ages we can see how the joke façade is introduced and how it gradually becomes more complicated. There is an increasing indirectness of expression; the child must find ways to gratify his impulses while disclaiming responsibility for them. Thus he proceeds from naughty acts to stories in which such acts are committed by others. Later these acts, even when attributed to fictitious characters, must be excused as comic mistakes. In addition, authority figures are made responsible for them.

Let us consider a sequence of dirty jokes of children from four through eleven in which we can observe the increasing complication of the joke façade. We may take the theme of excretory activities with which children are largely preoccupied in their dirty jokes. For a four-year-old it is a good dirty joke to shout at someone: "Hello, Doody!" or with slightly more subtle mockery: "Hello, Mr. Doody!" That the child finds this funny shows that he already has some misgiving about saying it. But in moments of weakened inhibition or strengthened impulse, which easily occur in his unstable inner economy, he can enjoy such a breakthrough of the forbidden without requiring any elaborate façade. However, there is already some indirectness in this seemingly blunt attack. Instead of precipitating his excreta on the victim, the child has substituted a verbal expression. He has embarked on the first stage of the development which will eventuate in the more complicated forms of wit.

Children over six introduce more elaboration into their jokes. We can see the difference between their requirements and those of younger children if we examine some of these more complex jokes and observe how younger children respond to them, reducing them to their bare essentials, and dispensing with the façade. Here is a joke told by a seven-year-old girl and taken over by her four-year-old brother in his own way. The girl tells me: "Once there was a little bear and he had to go to the bathroom. So he went up the first hill—" She illustrates this on her hand tracing a path up one finger, and explains that this should really be done on the other person's hand. "And he comes back and says, 'Mommy, there's people up there.'" The same thing is repeated for each of the five fingers. "He says, 'Mommy, I can't hold it any more.' Then you have a wet rag and you squeeze it on the other person's hand." The girl says that she learned this from her sister, two years older, and that she had tried it out on the maid the previous evening. She then adds: "Do you know what my little brother did? He thought the joke was so funny, he got a glass of water and threw it on the maid and she got all wet."

The two girls (seven and nine) present the joke of wetting someone with a verbal introduction which serves to conceal what is going to happen and also to justify it. The adults who impose so many restrictions on the child's freedom of excretion deserve to get urinated on. The responsibility of the child is reduced in that it is supposed to be the little bear and not the child who does the wetting. All this indirection is superfluous for the four-year-old brother. For him the whole joke is that his sister has unexpectedly poured water on the maid. Whatever inhibition he might have is overcome by the precedent which the older sister has established, and he makes what he probably considers an even funnier joke by throwing a larger amount of water on the victim. There is still some indirectness as water is substituted for urine. But he requires none of the excuses provided by the story, the pretense that it is the little bear, that the wetting is provoked by an impossible predicament.

We must of course be careful in speaking of a joke façade as being "required." At any age, a person might, given the proper circumstances, find it funny to pour water on someone else as simply as the four-year-old boy does. We should rather ask what gives the little bear story its appeal for his older sisters. Apparently it facilitates the overcoming of their greater inhibitions. These could also be overcome by an occasion in which everyone was behaving with reckless gaiety, which would enable them to act like their little brother. In the absence of such an occasion the story serves its purpose. The younger child has no need of it; for the older children it has a value under certain conditions. It makes them independent of the special occasions when there is a general relaxation of constraint, and gives them a device for surmounting inhibitions at will.

A five-year-old girl overhears her parents discussing dirty jokes and says that she will tell one. "A mother took her boy on the train and he made pee-pee all over the floor." This appears to be a simplified version of a joke which she has heard. Her father recalls one which was a favorite of his when he was about eight, and which he has retold saying that it was then his idea of a very good dirty joke. A boy named Kirk is taking his first train trip. He goes to the toilet and stays there a long time. The conductor keeps announcing station stops and finally calls out, "Dunkirk!" The boy calls back, "No, I haven't wiped myself yet." If we assume that this is the little girl's source for her dirty joke we can see how she has translated it into her own terms. The word play on "Dunkirk," and the boy's comic mistake in supposing that authorities

away from home will continue to supervise his toilet behavior just as they do at home, disappear. The combination of a journey and something funny about a child's
excretions means that the child cannot wait to get to the
toilet and urinates on the floor. That the child in her story
lacks the control which she herself presumably has contributes to the funny effect; and this may be underscored
by his being a boy and yet showing a weakness which she
would not have. In addition there is the pleasure in the
naughtiness of the child in the joke and the gratification
in fantasied looking at the little boy urinating. In the
Dunkirk joke there is a similar pleasure in evoking the
image of the little boy on the toilet, but this is not accepted as permissible in itself. The word play and comic
error of thought divert our attention from the cruder
satisfaction.

Here is a joke on a similar theme told by children between seven and eleven in which we can observe further
the more complicated façade which comes into use at these
ages. As told by the same seven-year-old girl from whom
we heard the little bear story: "Once there was a little
boy and he had to go to the bathroom. And he went over
to the teacher and said, 'I have to go to the bathroom.'
And the teacher said, 'Raise your hand to say your ABC.'
So the boy said, 'A B C D E F G H I J K L M N O Q
R S T U V W X Y Z.' And the teacher said, 'Where's
your P?' And the boy said, 'It ran down my pants.' "
Again the adult who makes unreasonable demands for
postponement is to blame for the child's wetting. The construction shows more complication and indirectness than
in the little bear joke: there is a play on words and described wetting replaces actual wetting. The aggressive
component is more interfered with as the child wets himself instead of someone else. There is also a degradation

of items of learning, an assertion of the identity of high and low. The teacher demands that the child turn his attention to the alphabet and stop thinking about his physical needs, but the child is able to demonstrate that there is a "P" even in the alphabet. A child in the predicament described might avoid saying "P" for fear he would do it, and also out of mocking compliance to the teacher who has demanded that he suppress the pee. However, the main impact for the children seems to derive from showing up the unreasonableness of the adults' demands and thus justifying the child's wetting.

The following joke, which was told by eleven-year-olds, shows a still more indirect treatment. "A lady was on a diet and she couldn't have any peas. So after five years she got off the diet, and she went to a restaurant and ordered dinner. She ordered a dish of peas and she said to the waiter, 'I haven't had a pea in five years.' And the waiter shouted, 'Hang onto the chandeliers, folks, there's going to be a flood!' " As in the alphabet joke, the excretory theme is here expressed in word play. But the excretory act is now further removed from reality. It does not occur, but is mistakenly apprehended by a character in the joke. This character serves a function which has been analyzed in connection with movie comedies as that of the comic onlooker.[54] Such a character misinterprets a harmless but ambiguous situation in a way which makes us see its naughty possibilities. At the same time we recognize that this is a misunderstanding and laugh at the one who has made the absurd mistake. It is he, not ourselves, who imagines the flood of urine. Our enjoyment of this fantasy is safeguarded by a double denial: the misbehavior does not occur and it is someone else who thinks of it. The sudden release of water becomes a non-existent event mistakenly anticipated by a fictitious character. Have we not come a long way from the little boy who threw water on the maid?

Allusion is a joke device which maximizes indirectness. One succeeds in making the hearer think of something without saying it oneself. The use of allusion implies a mastery of concealing and revealing which, as we shall see later, develops very gradually. Here is a joke told by an eleven-year-old boy which illustrates the allusive technique. "There's this man who has beer with his meal all the time. One day he opens the beer and tastes it and it tastes a little off. He sends it to the scientists to analyze. Four or five days later he gets a reply: 'Your horse has diabetes.' " Here the most important thing is left unsaid. We are, however, led to think of a perverse act, albeit committed unwittingly, the drinking of urine. This joke differs from those which we have just been discussing, and which deal with related matters, in that there is no mention of urinating or going to the bathroom in the manifest content. At the same time the meaning relates to a more forbidden act than any of the others.

Let us sum up the phases in development of the joke façade which we have observed. For a four-year-old, throwing water on someone is a joke. The only indirectness is the substitution of water for urine. A five-year-old tells a "dirty joke" in which a little boy makes pee-pee all over the floor. A description has been substituted for the act, and the character in the joke rather than the child himself becomes the performer. A seven-year-old tells the story of the little bear, in which the urgency to make water is justified by the unreasonable restrictions of the adults. The conflict with, and rebellion against authority enters into the joke content. An earlier element is retained in the actual wetting, which, however, is performed in a surprising way towards a victim who has been beguiled into foolish unwariness by the story. In the alphabet joke, the forbidden act is described rather than performed, the conflict with authority is more elaborated, the misbehaving child further justified, and the forbidden word is sanctioned by word play which gives it also a good meaning. In all the versions subsequent to the direct water throwing, the commission of the forbidden act is displaced onto a fictitious character. In "I haven't had a pea in five years," the forbidden act is not even committed by a fictitious character, but is only imagined by another character through a comic error of thought. In the beer joke a forbidden act has been, unwittingly, committed by a fictitious character, but the joke teller has not said one objectionable word; rather he has forced us to think what he has left unsaid. Thus increasingly intricate devices are used to circumvent growing inhibitions, to make possible the continued enjoyment of the forbidden without being disturbed by guilt.

Alleging that it is not I is a major defense of all fiction, joking or serious. While we get a vicarious satisfaction from identifying with fictitious characters, we retain a saving awareness that all the time it is someone else who does or experiences these things. In jokes we find the following progression in this disclaiming of responsibility: It is not I that does it; it is not I that says it; it is not I that thinks it. Thus in the little bear story there is the pretense that it is the little bear and not the child who *does* the wetting. In the alphabet joke it is the joke protagonists and not the teller who *mention* "P." In "I haven't had a pea in five years," it is a character in the joke who *thinks* of the forbidden thing. 'It is not I' is reenforced by 'It is not real,' which applies to all the instances given with the exception of the water throwing and the little bear story (and even there it is not real urine). Where word play is introduced there is a further mitigation of saying the forbidden in the semblance of saying something harmless ("P" is a letter of the alphabet which we are required to learn and say). A comic error of thought (such as the waiter's mistake) may serve to set the forbidden at yet a further remove from reality, since it occurs only as a mistaken notion of a foolish character. An allusive formulation insures immunity since nothing objectionable has been said. The teller may disclaim responsibility for what the hearer thinks.

II

Children of the latency period and older are apt to feel, or at least to say to an adult, that the jokes they have outgrown are those having to do with excretion. This may be partly insincere, partly a genuine illusion, partly an increased feeling that such jokes need a more elaborate façade. When I discussed with an eight-year-old girl what children consider funny at different ages, she confessed: "I used to think of nothing but my dirty behind when I was younger." A ten-year-old boy, when asked what younger children find funny, says: "They say, 'You're a doody.' You know what I mean? They always laugh at that." An eleven-year-old girl, in answer to the same question, says: "They think all these things about nature are funny. They say, 'Say Howdy Doody.' Then they say, 'Leave off the Howdy.'" Another eleven-year-old girl describes the sort of thing her five-year-old sister considers funny: "Little things that little kids think are funny, like: 'Diddledee doo, sitting on the toilet.' . . . Little kids make up really stupid things like that." These children are accurate observers of younger children and of their own past, while they may also be expressing present preoccupations which they are anxious to disclaim. The pleasure in excretion, disturbed by acquired feelings of shame and disgust, becomes the least socially admissible of physical enjoyments. While it remains a theme of joking at all ages, it is likely that such jokes are particularly susceptible to devaluation in retrospect and apt to be forgotten. Young children are still involved in the situation where adults supervise their toilet activities, so that excretory misbehavior expresses revolt. With age this factor becomes reduced. Also increasingly sexual relations become the crucial instance of the desirable and forbidden. It is interesting that jokes on this theme continue to be called "dirty." Inhibited sex tends to assume a regressive form and to be thought of as excretory.

Latency period children sometimes said to me that they knew dirty jokes but did not want to tell them, or would sometimes announce, anticipating possible disapproval, "This one is a little dirty—not really dirty." By prepuberty they are sometimes able to formulate the requirement that a dirty joke have an adequate façade. The eleven-year-old girl who rejects "Diddledee doo, sitting on the toilet" as "stupid," protests, probably in part insincerely, that she does not like dirty jokes. However, if she just happens to hear one, and "if it happens to be a good pun," she thinks it funny. She tells several dirty jokes (including genital as well as excretory themes) in which allusion or word play is employed. A friend of her mother's, who is in the advertising business, "called up and said she had a terrific slogan for such-and-such toilet paper: Tops for Bottoms. I think it's cute." It is the difference in form which distinguishes the "cute" from the "stupid" for this eleven-year-old. "Diddledee doo, sitting on the toilet" is an attempt to put the bad words into a song. Singing, or more often rhyming, serves as a mitigating device for children of about five. We shall examine the reasons for this presently. For the older child, this device becomes inadequate. "Tops for Bottoms" is a more complicated verbal gambit. It reveals an unexpected association to the stock slang superlative, "tops," and in so doing expresses anew the persistent tendency to bring together the high and low. It exposes advertising as an attempt to glorify unworthy objects, and breaks through the euphemisms which the advertiser applies to such a product. This "terrific slogan" is one that can never be used, and as we see this we are made to realize the disingenuousness of advertising. Thus with great conciseness more is expressed here than in the younger child's song about sitting on the toilet. The toilet theme is used as a means of degradation for the purpose of social criticism. Conversely, the exposure of conventions as dishonest permits the expression of the forbidden.

III

The alternation between concealing and revealing is a major aspect of jokes. A joke has a point which must first be concealed and then exposed. The skill of the joke teller consists to a large extent in managing this transition. We shall see presently that it is a difficult one for children to master. The little drama of concealing and then revealing something is implicitly an exhibitionistic performance. While this is a formal aspect of all jokes which have a concealed point, exposure of oneself or of others may also provide the specific subject matter of jokes. Before considering concealment as a general technical device, let us first examine the different ways in which children deal with sexual exposure as a theme for joking.

For very young children simply exposing themselves may be funny. They have for the moment overcome an inhibition whose force is weak and fluctuating. A child of five or six may use joke telling as a facilitation for abandonment of shame, and may kick his legs in the air or pull up his clothes. He thus reverts from the more indirect expression of the verbal joke to its underlying meaning as an exposure of the forbidden.

From self-exposure the next step is the joking exposure of the other person. The two acts are of course intimately related. In the child's expectation self-exposure should lead to corresponding behavior on the part of the other person. However, the exposure of the other, without exposure of the self, is usually predicated on a stronger inhibition, and on the assumption of the other's unwillingness. The exposure of the other thus takes on a hostile tone; resentment at being frustrated and a wish to unmask and to degrade enter into it. In its simplest form such exposure is exemplified in little boys' pulling up little girls' skirts. As more restraint takes effect, words are substituted for acts. We then find the joking rhymes in which another person is invited to expose himself or alleged to have done so. A six-year-old boy tells one of these, explaining that the children "say it to anyone they don't like. You say to someone called Billy:

> Billy was the king of France
> He pulled down his underpants
> Right in the middle of the Sunday dance."

The fine pretensions of the victim are derided: You think you're so great but you have a backside too.

In the next step it is neither the child himself nor the person he addresses but a third person who is exposed. The same six-year-old boy gives an instance of this, in another joking rhyme:

Hi-ho Silver everywhere
Tonto lost his underwear
Said Tonto: "Me don't care
Me go get another pair."

A person described in the joke now appears as the one who exhibits himself, and both the joke teller and the hearer can laugh at him. A more complicated joke, told by nine- and ten-year-old children, similarly displaces the forbidden act to a character in the joke. As told by a nine-year-old girl: "This girl was walking along the street and she met a man. And he said, 'If you stand on your head ten times, I'll give you ten dollars.' So she stood on her head once, twice, three times. . . . Then she went home and showed her mother the ten dollars. And her mother said, 'Where did you get it?' And the girl said, 'I met a man and he gave it to me.' And the mother said, 'You didn't take from a man?' And the girl said, 'I stood on my head ten times to get it.' And the mother said, 'You naughty girl! He saw your underpants.' And the girl said, 'I fooled him—I didn't wear any.' " The construction here is more elaborate than in the rhyme in which Tonto lost his underwear. The little girl in the joke who seemingly does not know that it is naughtier to exhibit herself than to let her underpants be seen is committing a comic error of thought, or in a pseudo-naive way showing mocking compliance to the mother. It is as if she says: You told me not to let anyone see my underpants, so I was careful to take them off. The more complicated treatment of the theme thus contains more than the description of the forbidden act. It includes spiting the forbidding authority. We have seen this also in the more advanced treatments of the wetting theme.

To sum up these phases, the child first jokingly exhibits himself, momentarily overcoming an unstable inhibition. Next he may use verbal joking as a preliminary to facilitate the same act, achieving an initial weakening of inhibition by the verbal joke. Becoming aware that others have resistances to being exposed, he may expose them against their will. But as he develops inhibitions against such rude behavior, he substitutes a verbal attack in which he alleges that the other has exposed himself. Finally the self-exposure is performed by a character in the joke at whom teller and hearer can laugh together. This is then susceptible to further complication as the action described may take the form of a comic error or may be combined with mockery of forbidding authorities.

IV

Joking involves exposure even where exposure is not its manifest theme. The joke has a point which must first be concealed and then revealed. Implicitly the point represents an interesting part of the body.[55] The joke teller by first veiling the point teases and intrigues the hearer. After having built up the other's expectancy, the teller reveals the point and is gratified if it rouses admiration. While the joke substitutes something heard for something seen, the underlying idea of looking is expressed in: "See the point?" Artistry in the joke and virtuosity in its telling are largely related to achieving an optimal relation between concealing and revealing. If the point is either too obvious or too obscure the joke is incompletely successful. Children have great difficulty in mastering the art of concealment. They tend to err either on the side of too much or too little. This is in part related to the unstable balance between their inhibitions and impulses. But they are also unsure about what the other person sees. They may alternately attribute to him an impossible omniscience or suppose him to be blinded by the most transparent device.

To understand children's difficulties about concealment and about giving adequate clues for discovery it is useful to observe the kind of guessing games they play as various ages. Even earlier than guessing games there is the playful concealment which evokes so much laughter from the infant, the peekaboo game. Here the child is concealed by courtesy of the adult's pretense not to see him. The mother puts a cloth over the child's face, and asks: "Where's baby?" in simulated puzzlement, while the child delightedly stays still in assumed invisibility. Four-year-old children may still hide repeatedly in the same place while the adult pretends to look for them and finally finds them.[56] A similar thing may be observed in guessing games as played by four-year-olds. Larry, who has drawn a picture of a shoe, after telling me what it is, asks me to pretend that I do not know and to try to guess. He helpfully informs me when my guesses are coming close, and is delighted when I finally guess it is a shoe. Four-year-old children have great difficulty in maintaining real concealment. The teacher leads them in a game in which they are supposed to say, "I'm thinking of someone with a green shirt," and so on, giving clues from which the others may guess the person's identity. The children repeatedly point to the one they are describing. In another variant of the game, the teacher asks questions to discover the identity of someone the children have agreed on while she was out of the room. When she asks if it is someone wearing blue dungarees, which would apply to half the children present, they hasten to tell her, "Yes, it's Johnny," despite her urging them not to give it away too quickly.

In guessing games of five-year-olds one may observe a reversal of this. From inadequate concealment they turn to an excess. So they may play a game in which one says,

"I'm thinking of a number," and the others are required to guess. While at this age they are incompletely aware of how many numbers there are, there are still a lot to choose from. In asking a question which provides so little clue to the answer, they show more concern for concealment than for the possibility of being discovered. Where the four-year-old too readily precipitated discovery, the five-year-old makes it nearly impossible. Probably he underestimates the difficulty for others to find out what he is concealing, and is testing whether he can really conceal something.

The child's belief that he can conceal things from the adults develops only gradually. It must contend with the early belief in the adults' omniscience. The child's motivation for concealment also increases with age. It is related to his awareness of the adults' disapproval and to the increasing pressure of impulses which actually or as he imagines would call down severe retribution. We may suppose that from four to five, with the intensification of oedipal motives, the child's need for concealment increases. There is also an increased impetus towards repression following this phase; concealment from external observation is extended into concealment from internal awareness. A further motivation for concealment proceeds from the child's reaction to his increased awareness of the adults' concealing things from him. He wants to turn the tables and himself conceal something. We have seen how this wish contributes to the liking for joking riddles.

The jokes of latency period children show a peculiar polarization in respect to concealing and revealing. While in some there is an excess of concealment, in others the point is too obviously exposed from the start. The riddles which we discussed in the last chapter involve excessive concealment in two ways. Too few clues are given for ascertaining the correct answer and the underlying sexual or aggressive theme is not made manifest at all. As to the first point, the joking riddle admits of many answers which, however, the person asking it will reject. For instance, we might guess that the moron jumped off the Empire State Building because his girl did not love him any more. Nothing in the question excludes this answer, but the riddler will reject it. He has a trick answer to which the question gives no adequate clue. Knowing the conventions of such riddles, the person asked will usually not propose any answer which does not have a trick to it. But there are also several possible trick answers among which the riddler will accept only the one he happens to have chosen. The tendency to give too few clues is illustrated in a riddle invented by a ten-year-old girl: "What has teeth?" After one has guessed a comb, a saw, etc., all of which she rejects, she gives the answer: "A good law." Her teacher has remarked that a good law has to have teeth in it, and this has given her the idea for her riddle. But this is a kind of guessing game which resembles the five-year-olds' "Guess what number I'm thinking of." The chance of guessing is slight because the possibilities are inadequately delimited. The revealing of the answer is at the discretion of the one who asks. The same ten-year-old girl asks: "What does seven and nine make?" "Sixteen." "No, seventy-nine. . . . Then you ask again, 'What does seven and nine make?' The victim answers, 'Seventy-nine.' You answer, 'Sixteen.' " The wish to frustrate the "victim" is evident. What is an acceptable answer is determined by the arbitrary decision of the questioner. In this the child appears to be giving a parody of the adults, who conceal things, do not give the child a chance to find out for himself, and decide what is acceptable in a way that often seems arbitrary.[57]

Many of the joking riddles, as we have observed, deal with sexual and aggressive themes. These themes appear from an analysis of the joke and are sometimes present in the children's conscious associations, but they are not expressed in the manifest content. Take for instance, "Why does the fireman wear red suspenders?—To hold his pants up." As we have seen, the children's associations are about what would happen if the pants fell down, and so on. But this is excluded from the joke content; it remains concealed. The child presents a harmless façade and keeps the less harmless associations to himself. In many cases, however, we have to do with repression rather than suppression. The child is not aware of the sexual or aggressive meaning. These jokes, which latency period children are so fond of, in which there is a forbidden motive which is not brought to the surface, are apt to seem insipid to adolescents and adults. For them a joke must end by revealing what it initially conceals in order to have an adequate impact. But presumably for latency period children concealment by itself has a greater value, so that they feel less the requirement of shifting to exposure.

However, another group of preferred latency period jokes show just the opposite. They provide inadequate concealment of the point, which, at least to the adult, is exposed from the start. It seems likely that to some extent this is even for the child a pretended concealment as in the earlier peekaboo games. Only here it is the child who assumes the rôle which the adult played earlier in pretending that something is hidden which is plainly visible. We have discussed, in Chapter 2, the series of jokes about the mother and the little boy named Heinie, which are such favorites with children of about nine. That "Heinie" is a boy's name may serve on the first hearing to put off the awareness of its other meaning (behind). But even this is questionable for children who have never known a boy named Heinie. Certainly on hearing other Heinie jokes (and these are told endlessly with slight variations), the child sees through the flimsy concealment from the start. In a version given by a nine-year-old girl the semblance of using a real name is dropped: for "Heinie" she substitutes "Tooshie" which also means "behind," but which is not a proper name. She says: "There was this boy and his name was Tooshie. It's really a dirty one. One day his mother went into a store to buy some toilet paper. She said to the man, 'May I please have some toilet paper to wipe my Tooshie?' " There is still an ambiguity here in that "my Tooshie" means both the boy and the mother's behind. For the child, the joke gains its effect from this double meaning which provides for the mother's unwitting self-exposure. However, there is no real double meaning in the use of "Tooshie" as a name. In telling us, "There was this boy and his name was Tooshie," the girl is saying in effect: Let's pretend that Tooshie could be a boy's name and forget for the moment that it means something else. The other meaning of "Tooshie" is then brought out by the last line. We are to pretend that when the mother speaks of wiping her tooshie with toilet paper we suddenly recall the usual meaning of "tooshie."

At times the child seems to overestimate the effectiveness of a concealment device which appears transparent to the adult. The same nine-year-old girl tells the joke about the woman taking a bath who has a little dog named "Freeshow." For the adult the machinery of the joke is so exposed to view at the start that what we are apt to find comic is that the child could suppose we do not see what she is getting at. But the girl tells us, "This is like a riddle." She seems to feel that it will be really difficult for us to discover the hidden meaning. By saying that

"Freeshow," is a name she feels that she prevents us from seeing any other meaning in it. The special feelings about names which we discussed earlier enter in here. While children have a strong urge to find meanings in proper names, they also learn that they should inhibit this. The Freeshow joke assumes this inhibition: if it is a name we will not look for a meaning in it. The girl is concerned that we get the full effect of the exposure when she finally produces it. After telling that the woman ran outside calling, "Freeshow! Freeshow!" she adds: "And all the people thought she meant it was a free show because she was all undressed." She wants to be sure that we fully appreciate the meaning of "a free show" and that we get the picture of the woman "all undressed." Having embarked on a story in which exposure is the manifest theme, she apparently wants to extract the maximum effect from it. Perhaps the verbal description is not a wholly satisfying substitute for things actually seen, and she tries to intensify the impact by repeating the key words. Such a joke with its transparency and emphasis on revealment is the opposite of the joking riddles where the verbal construction gives inadequate clues to the answer and the sexual theme remains veiled throughout.

We have seen the two following combinations of revealing and concealing: intensive concealment in verbal form combined with similar concealment of a sexual or aggressive theme, and inadequate concealment in both respects. Two other combinations are possible. We may have a high degree of concealment in verbal form but exposure of the forbidden motive. This occurs in those joking riddles where the answer makes explicit a sexual or aggressive point. (What's the difference between an oyster and a baby?—The oyster makes his bed in the ocean, and the baby makes an ocean in his bed.) The remaining possibility would be one where the verbal structure is very transparent, but the content harmless. But this would hardly be a joke. The main preferences of latency period children seem to be for the first two types, either of extreme concealment in structure and of content, or of too ready exposure in both respects (as in the Heinie and Freeshow jokes).

What seems for the most part absent in latency period jokes is the transition from concealing to revealing which characterizes well constructed and skillfully told jokes of adults. In the latter the construction, without assuming the character of a guessing game, adequately veils the aggressive or sexual motive which will at the appropriate moment come out and produce its impact through a surprise effect. How shall we explain the fact that in contrast to this the sexual jokes preferred by latency period children tend to be of the Freeshow type? It would seem that they want to avoid a real surprise, the drastic and dramatic shift from not seeing to seeing. Instead they play the game of only pretending not to see. If the joke is to have a sexual point they prefer to keep it in view, at least out of the corner of their eye, from the start. Where there is real concealment and more surprise, as in adult jokes, we have a sudden release of an impulse from inhibition. To be able to enjoy this we must feel rather confident of not being overwhelmed by such a break-through. We must trust that we will not be carried away by the impulse, that its gratification will be confined to the moment of the joke. Still, even in adults the surprise and suddenness which are important for the joke's impact occasion a fleeting initial terror. There is a tendency to marshal increasing inhibitions for a moment, until we realize that we are not seriously threatened.[58] The latency period child maintains a more inflexible set of inhibitions and is less able playfully to suspend them. A sudden break-through of impulse carries for him the threat of being overwhelmed; the initial terror would not be so readily dissipated. Thus he prefers a familiar Heinie joke to one which would unexpectedly penetrate his inhibitions. The overly revealing jokes are thus related to the same motive as the overly concealing ones: the fear of being overwhelmed by impulse. In the overly revealing joke the child can see what is coming and has time to assimilate it. In the overly concealing joke he wards off the awareness of dangerous impulses throughout.

V

The joking expression of aggression follows a somewhat different line of development than the treatment of sexual themes. We have reconstructed the series of modes of sexual exposure: I expose myself; I expose you; I expose a third person whom you and I can laugh at together. With the expression of hostility we find: first, I attack you; second, I divert the attack to a third person for our common amusement; finally, I attack myself. In this last, where the joke is at one's own expense, aggression has been most interfered with. But in making jokes about one's own embarrassments or absurd mistakes, one recaptures the possibility of self-exposure. The exposure is mitigated and made permissible by presenting oneself in a ridiculous light.

Aggression against the person directly before us may be mitigated in two ways, by displacing the attack to another victim or by disclaiming one's own responsibility for the attack. Children seem to prefer the latter alternative, of which there are numerous variants. One of the earliest of these is the rhymed insult, which is popular with five-year-olds. The following are instances:

Baby, baby! Stick your head in gravy!

I'm the king of the castle, and you're a dirty old rascal!

What is the function of rhyme in these joking attacks? I would suggest that the first rhyming word has the effect of compelling the utterance of the second, thus reducing the speaker's responsibility. As we shall see in a moment, a more advanced maneuver consists in inducing the victim to utter the first rhyming word, to which the joker then joins the rhymed insult. Once the first word has been spoken, it is as if the rhyming word has been commanded. There is a further reduction of responsibility in the use of a learned formula: The words are not my own. Moreover the rhyme is apt to induce other children to take it up; the attacker will cease to be alone. It should be added that rhymes are often in themselves funny to young children. Children of three, for instance, may laugh simply at finding two words that rhyme or a word that rhymes with a name. Thus the rhyme affords a façade of harmless joking to facilitate the expression of hostility in the rhymed insult. The amusement with rhymes illustrates the early pleasure in playing with words better than puns. Young children enjoy the discovery of sound similarities, but when a shift of meaning is forced on them they are more apt to be distressed, as we have seen. It has been told of Keats that at an early age he used to reply to anything that was said to him by producing a rhyming word and laughing.[59] These early reactions are later reversed. Rhyme becomes mainly a means of serious poetry, intensifying rather than reducing emotion, while it is the shift of meanings which becomes the major verbal gambit of jokes.

The use of rhyme and also melody to mitigate verbal

impropriety may be observed in the following. Two five-year-old girls were fond of singing to the tune of Brahms' lullaby all the dirty words they knew, which they rhymed to the best of their ability: "Bottom plus, uterus, genitals and penus. . . ." In addition to the rhyme, the melody which they probably knew was a lullaby, that is a song associated with children in the most seemly way, glossed over the naughty words. Conversely the naughty words debunked the sentiment of the lullaby.

Returning to techniques of attack against the hearer of the joke, there is a series of devices by which the victim is increasingly forced to be the agent of the attack against himself. He may be maneuvered into the position of asking for it. The Pinch-me joke is an instance of this. In other cases the victim is induced to say a word with which an insult is rhymed.

"What's twelve and twelve?"
"Twenty-four."
"Shut your mouth and say no more."

"What's eight and eight?"
"Sixteen."
"Stick your head in kerosene, wipe it off with ice-cream, and show it to the king and queen."

In these, as in the Pinch-me joke, the respondent is rebuked for thinking he is smart; giving the answer precipitates an attack. The first rhyming word is taken as a cue and a command for the verbal hostilities which follow. The respondent is made to feel that he set it off, he asked for it. These jokes seem to be popular with children of about seven. They show an advance over "Baby, baby, stick your head in gravy," in that the attacker has further reduced his responsibility, forcing the victim to assume part of it.

Puns replace rhymes in the following instance where the victim again is made to assume part of the responsibility for the attack upon him.

> "Which would you rather be, a fountain, a tree, or a lollipop?"
> "A fountain."
> "You drip!—Now which would you rather be, a tree or a lollipop?"
> "A tree."
> "You sap!—Now which would you rather be, a lollipop or a lollipop?"
> "All right, a lollipop."
> "You sucker!"

Here there is a further inculpation of the victim who is maneuvered into choosing to be what is the cryptic equivalent of a "drip," a "sap," or a "sucker." The implication "You asked for it" is strengthened by the pretense of giving the victim a choice. (This joke was told by a ten-year-old.)

The last step in maneuvering the victim into attacking himself consists in getting him to utter the insult. We find this in a joke discussed earlier where the child instructs us that whatever kind of a lock he says he is we should say we are that kind of key. At the end of a series which is intended to induce an unthinking automatism in the victim,[60] we reply to "I'm a don lock" with "I'm a don key." Where the victim is induced to confess that he is a donkey, the transition is completed from 'I attack you' to 'You attack yourself.' While this expresses an interference with aggression, in the disclaiming of responsibility, it also interferes with counter aggression since the victim must blame himself for having fallen into the trap. He is thus disarmed; the attacker gets away with it.

A related form of joking consists in using a person's

words against him, taking them in a sense opposed to his wishes. This also shifts the responsibility: It is you, not I who said it. Twisting the other person's words is a favored mode of attack against adults. It can serve a variety of motives, alleging that the person whose words are thus turned has asked to be attacked, that he has acknowledged his immorality, exposed his stupidity, or sanctioned impermissible behavior. We have discussed a number of instances of this in Chapter 2. Here is a further example, in which the word for which the adult is made responsible is not uttered but exposed to view in print. Ten-year-old Alfred found a copy of *Punch* lying on my table. He read the title and proceeded to punch me, saying: "I'm a law-abiding citizen, I follow all the signs."

The modifications of 'I attack you' may, as we have seen, proceed in two directions: 'It is not I who attack you' and 'It is not you I attack.' Children to begin with seem to prefer the former alternative. They do not want to be deprived of their victim, but rather to make the attack safe by various disclaimers of responsibility. Interference with the direction of the attack, diverting it from the other person, may end in turning it inwards against oneself. This would be a much more drastic and painful modification of the impulse than merely veiling it under the pretense 'It is not I that does it or says it.'

The strenuous effort to avoid turning aggression against the self may also be observed in the early moral development of children. When children of three or four are taught certain rules in nursery school their initial tendency is to apply them to the other children. The rule about taking turns on the tricycle, for instance, is used to give a tone of righteousness to a child's demand that another relinquish the tricycle he wants, but is not accepted as limiting his possession once he obtains it. Thus the child continues to attack whoever stands in his way, but has acquired a new justification: It is not simply I that demand it—it is the rule. Struggling against the efforts of the adults to get him to control his own impulses, he prefers to try to control those of others. Similar tendencies may be observed in a more complicated form in latency period children, who are fond of making up rules. The main tenor of these rules is to restrict the activities of the other children and to justify the imposition of penalties on them. By this moralized aggression against others they attempt to divert the attacks of conscience directed against themselves. Latency period children have a peculiarly intense intolerance of being put in the wrong or shown to be stupid. The preferred defense against such painful admissions is to demonstrate that someone else is stupid or blameworthy. Thus the aggressive impulse towards others is reenforced by the underlying feeling: If I did not attack you, I might have to attack myself. We have seen how this works in the joking riddles where the child asking the riddle proves at the same time that he is smart and the other is stupid.

While a joke at one's own expense is a difficult achievement, jokes in which a third person is made the butt of both teller and hearer occur quite early. In these, aggression is still turned outward, but is displaced from the person addressed to a more remote target. In some cases such a joke may be an effort to mitigate preceding hostilities between the teller and hearer. Four-year-old Chris feels angry and resentful because he sees his friend Ben whispering with another child. He goes over and gives Ben a hard push, knocking him down. Ben says, "I hate you." Chris, becoming conciliatory, says: "Ben, you know what? On a summer day a bunny went out and tripped over a tree. Isn't that funny?" Ben agrees that it is and they are friends again. In Chris's little joke it is a third person, the bunny, who has fallen down, and besides he wasn't pushed, he tripped. Thus Chris tries to deny his own aggressiveness, and provides an outside victim at whom he and his friend can laugh together.

Older children sometimes admit that they tell their younger brothers or sisters jokes to divert them after having attacked them. A ten-year-old boy says about his little brother: "When I do something to him and don't want him to tell my mother, I tell him dirty jokes." "What jokes do you tell him?" "About when we were at camp and we played Tararaboomdeay and bumped our behinds together. It's not very nice, but it's the healthiest way. Otherwise my father's belt would be worn out before now." Even where such hostilities between teller and hearer have not occurred so overtly, the joking direction of aggression against a third person tends for the moment to increase positive feelings between the joke participants.

In adolescence there is a reduction of the effort so strenuously maintained in latency to deny that the comical or foolish person could be oneself. We may recall the thirteen-year-old girl who, in talking about the moron, said with affectionate teasing to her friend: "I didn't say it was you—it could be me." Similarly another girl of the same age said she liked jokes in which characters made mistakes of the sort she might make. "You'll laugh when you make your own mistake yourself." How shall we explain this difference between the latency period child and the adolescent? I think that it may be interpreted in part in terms of a changing attitude towards one's own impulses. Foolish behavior is impulsive behavior (as we have seen, for instance, in the characterization of the moron). The latency period child has to a large extent repudiated impulses in favor of smartness, skill, and control. With puberty, intensified impulses not only become threatening but begin to assume many positive values. When the adolescent laughs at his own mistakes it is because he sees himself as not completely controlled, as an impulsive person and does not entirely mind showing himself in this light. He makes himself attractive as a creature of impulse, one who could also satisfy another's impulses. This is not to deny that he feels chagrined at his mistakes or disturbed at his lack of control. But the growing positive overtones of impulsiveness counteract these feelings to a greater extent than formerly.

Children are apt to make a joke of intentional mistakes before they are able to laugh at unintentional ones. A child of three or four, having fallen by accident, will make a joke of it by subsequently throwing himself down on purpose. He thus turns passivity into activity and implies that if accidents happen it is because he makes them happen. The intentional accident is a means of undoing the unintentional one. Children of four and five already show considerable aptitude for the joking production of intentional mistakes, especially when these may be annoying to others. Another factor enters in here: they have learned that accidents or mistakes are excusable. Thus four-year-olds, when told by the teacher to wash their faces, may pretend to make a foolish mistake by washing the face in the mirror instead.

Intentional mistakes or the simulated ineptitude of the comedian imply a real mastery on the part of the actor: he only pretends to lose control. To be able to laugh at one's unintentional mistakes, to recover from the chagrin of a real loss of control, is usually a more difficult achievement. Telling about one's mistakes afterwards, as against laughing when they occur, provides a rectification by subsequent mastery which, on the verbal level, corresponds to the young child's throwing himself down intentionally after an accidental fall. By turning a mishap into an anecdote one voluntarily repeats the experience in imagination: choosing to make it happen, one transforms passivity into activity. Verbal skill in telling contributes to the undoing of the previous ineptitude. The sense of detachment in being able to tell about one's past discomfiture reverses the impression of failure in control. The unpleasantness of the mishap is further compensated by the amused reactions of others to the good story one has made of it.

When the joke teller, raconteur, or comedian offers himself as an object for laughter, he revives on a higher level the pleasure of exhibiting himself. It is as if he pays for the forbidden exhibition, and wards off punishment for it, by at the same time attacking himself, showing himself as foolish and harmless. The comedian or the person who makes a joke at his own expense thus compensates himself by the exhibition for which he gains immunity. There is, however, another form of joke at one's own expense, in which the factor of exhibition is dispensed with or ceases to be essential. This is what Freud called humor. We are able to laugh at our own misfortunes. Our satisfaction derives from a triumph over distress and does not require the appreciation of an audience. Where the comedian offers himself to the gaze of others in the guise of childish ineptitude, the humorist looks on himself as a child and on his troubles as childishly unimportant. The expression of aggression in laughing at oneself is the most indirect and shows the greatest diversion from joking hostility against another. If we consider the persons involved in the joke, whether as agents, victims, or spectators, we then have the following series: I attack you;

I attack a third person for your and my amusement; I attack myself for your amusement; I attack myself (or utilize my having been attacked) for my own amusement. The sequence exhibits a progressive interference with aggression.

Except for the kind of humor whose sanction is internal, sharing the joke with someone else is essential for enjoying it. The response of the other person assures us that the forbidden motives which we express are permissible. The various devices which we have analyzed, by means of which sexual and aggressive themes are disguised, serve equally to avoid inner censorship and to disarm that of the hearer. If he laughs the joke is a success; if not, we feel the shame and guilt which the joking expression aimed at warding off.[61]

VI

In this chapter we have traced the processes by which jokes become more complicated as various devices become necessary to guard sexual and aggressive pleasures from the encroachment of inhibitions. For children under six, in whom these inhibitions are unstable and subject to frequent spontaneous lapses, the mitigation afforded by the joke façade is not required. For older children this façade becomes useful as a means for overriding more persistent inhibitions. We have seen how from the age of four to prepuberty they advance from making a joke of simply throwing water on someone else to a joke in which an improper excretory act is mistakenly anticipated by a character in the joke ("I haven't had a pea in five years"). We noted the progressive disclaiming of responsibility in the joker as he implies that it is not he who does or says or even thinks the forbidden thing. We have analyzed concealment and exhibition both as a topic for joking (in jokes about sexual exposure) and as a technical aspect of all jokes which have a concealed point. In jokes dealing with sexual exposure we found the series of stages: I expose myself; I expose you; I expose a third person whom you and I can laugh at together. As to the technical procedure of revealing a concealed point, we found that this is not mastered till after the latency period. Children in the latency period, fearing to be surprised and overwhelmed by their impulses, favor jokes in which the forbidden meaning remains concealed throughout or the opposite: jokes where the sexual point is apparent from the start. In hostile joking, we observed two main methods of mitigation: disclaiming responsibility for the attack and diverting the direction of the attack. Children tend to prefer the former. They do not want to be deprived of their victim, and fear on a less conscious level that by redirection of the hostile impulse they may have to turn it against themselves. In children's hostile jokes there are many devices for disclaiming responsibility, notably maneuvering the victim into assuming it. The capacity to make a joke at one's own expense increases with the onset of adolescence, when, among other things, it is compensated by some pleasure in seeing oneself as a foolish, impulsive person. In the redirection of aggression against oneself, there is also a recapturing of the pleasure of self exhibition; this becomes harmless and permissible as one exhibits oneself in a ridiculous light.

In the development of the more complicated forms of joking, two processes keep pace with one another: the child's increasing scruples about simple release of impulse, and his progressive acquisition of techniques for circumventing these scruples. The mastery of these devices brings not only pleasure in virtuosity, but momentary triumph over inhibition, and the response of others.

CHAPTER 5

Understanding the Joke

I

LISTENING to grownups, children hear many things which they do not understand. Sometimes they feel puzzled; they have a vague awareness of something beyond their grasp. Often they put their own construction on what they have heard, not realizing till much later that they have not understood correctly.

Few things, I think, evoke so convincingly the atmosphere of our own childhood, so strange but not entirely beyond recapturing, as the recollection of our childhood misunderstandings. When I was a child, I used to hear a maid of European origin talk about the "old country." I imagined that this was a country that existed before I was born and that had now ceased to exist; it was something the grownups knew about that I could never know. Recently I heard about a little boy who had been told something about genetics and who later remarked wonderingly: "You know, they say I'm the way I am because of my blue jeans." In their solitary reading, children often attach their own meanings to words; this is facilitated by their also not knowing the correct pronunciation. So a friend of mine used to think that "sundry" meant "dried by the sun." She had first come across it in the *National Geographic*—some such phrase as "various and sundry places," and the word had called up images of luminous, parched deserts.

Here is the way two six-year-old boys have understood the term "double-header," which they have picked up from the talk of older boys or of their fathers. Karl tells me that he has made up a joke: "Why did the moron go to the model shop to get a head to paste on the Dodgers stand?" (He explains, in answer to my question, that he means a model of a head.) He then gives the answer: "So they would have a double-header." Bob, overhearing this, asks somewhat patronizingly: "Do you know what a double-header is, Karly?" Karl replies: "A Dodger with two heads." Bob enlightens him: "No, two people who own the Dodgers. They're two people, so they have two heads." Each of these boys has supplied his own meaning to what he has heard and is unaware of any misunderstanding.[62]

However, there are also times when children realize that they have not understood. Many children say that they do not think the things their parents laugh at are funny because they do not understand them. Sometimes when a child tries to reconstruct what he has heard, the grownups laugh at him, and yet do not enlighten him. He may adhere to his own version, and yet know that there is something wrong with it. Thus five-year-old Lenny tells me the following joke: "Once a girl was getting off a train and someone says, 'How.' And she says, 'I know how—boo!'" I ask him where he got his joke, and he says: "I thought Daddy was saying it one day and that's how I got the joke. But I misunderstood him." "Then what did he really say?" "How do I know if I misunderstood him?" A little girl who is listening laughs, and Lenny says: "That must be a joke too if you laugh." Lenny's teacher informs me that Lenny has proudly told his joke several times in class and laughed over it; he has explained to the other children that "how" is Indian language. Apparently Lenny gets satisfaction out of mimicking his father to the best of his ability, even though he knows he cannot reproduce his father's performance exactly. Perhaps, too, he is pleased to mystify the other children as he was mystified by the father's incomprehensible joke.

I would guess that what Lenny's father told was the following current adult joke: An Indian chief's daughter goes to Vassar and comes back pregnant. As she gets off the train, she greets her father: "How." The father says, "Never mind how. Who?" This last (if my guess is correct) Lenny translated into: "I know how—boo!" Lenny may have had an inkling that his father's joke had something to do with procreation. "I know how—boo!" would then mean: I know how it's done, and it's very frightening. Lenny produced an original funny story in which a farmer goes into a red field and, having swallowed his seeds, has to plant himself by burying himself in the ground. When the teacher, reading a story book to the children, showed them a picture of a net full of fish, Lenny jumped up and ran away in mock terror. We may infer that one of the things that frightens Lenny about the sexual activity of his parents is how the father, having entered the mother (becoming buried in the red field, caught in the net), can extricate himself. He fails to understand not only the solution to the father's joke but the solution to the father's sexual hazards. His own version of the joke may then express an attempt to deny his failure to understand as well as his fright. Instead of being mystified and scared, he asserts that he knows and can scare others: "I know how—boo!"

II

The understanding of jokes involves a variety of factors. A verbal joke is a complicated construction; children, in learning it, may respond to one component of it but not to another. Thus a joke may combine certain obvious features (such as description of outlandish behavior), which children may enjoy, with other features that are more subtle (word play, comic error of thought), which they miss. In an earlier essay I tried to show how children use certain jokes without responding to the word play in them.[63] Now I should like to consider another aspect of joke comprehension: being able to distinguish between joking and nonjoking discourse.

As adults we recognize two distinct realms of discourse, the serious and the joking. What is appropriate in one is not appropriate in the other. If one fails to take a joke jokingly one makes a mistake, and if one intrudes joking into serious matters one may be rebuked, though there are various legitimate transitions from the serious to the joking. These are social conventions built around alternative psychological possibilities, on the one hand of making sense in a logical, realistic way, on the other of indulging in absurdity. Children learn only gradually to distinguish these two realms of discourse. They are in the process of acquiring logic and a sense of reality. While they can easily break away from the demands of reason on their own initiative and enjoy fantasy or nonsense, it is not always clear to them when others, especially their elders, make this shift. When grownups tease children by dealing with something in a joking way, the children may be baffled or hurt. They feel that the grownups represent the demands of reason, and they have then to learn that there are times when the grownups themselves suspend these demands. Joking has its own rules which run counter to those of reasonable discourse. The child who is busy learning to master the realistic and logical frequently protests that jokes are stupid, that they do not make sense. Only gradually does he come to realize that in a joke it is not only permitted but required not to make sense in the logical way.

In investigating children's ability to distinguish between joking and nonjoking discourse, I presented them with a series of joking riddles. I told each child that I would like to tell him some jokes that I had heard from other children and to see whether he knew them and whether he thought them funny. I asked him if he could think of alternative answers to the joking riddles, proposed to him nonjoking answers and asked whether those answers would be all right and if not, why. This latter question was particularly revealing of the extent to which the child had mastered the conventions of the joke.

Let us take a particular riddle and see how the children reacted to it. There is one about a man locked in a house, of which I had learned numerous variants from different children. In one version, we are asked how the man lived, and told that he ate the dates from the calendar and got water from the springs of the bed. Or we are asked how he got out, and told that he took a key from the piano and unlocked the door (or played the piano till he found the right key) ; or that he knocked himself out; or that he had a bat and ball—three strikes and you're out. Or it was a holy church, so he got out through the holes. Yet another version pictures the man locked out of the house and asks how he got in. He ran around until he was all in. In its latent meaning, the riddle of the locked house relates to major sexual questions: how does the baby live in the womb? how does it get out? how does it get in in the first place? how does the man get into the woman? and how does he get out again? In addition it has for many children the association of being confined to their rooms as a punishment, and so evokes lively and urgent fantasies of escape. In some cases, it is associated with the child's fantasy of withdrawing to his room in angry resentment against the parents; here the question is how to live in this self-imposed confinement. In other instances, the associated problem seems to be that of being closed up in the house with the mother and wanting to "strike out" on one's own. Thus the problem jokingly proposed is one which the children feel for many reasons a strong urge to solve.

The form of this riddle which I presented to the children proposed a double question, how the man in the locked house could live and how he could get out. If the child had not heard the riddle before, I asked him to guess the answer. After one or other of the conventional answers had been given, either by the child or by me, I would propose the following: "Someone told me that he could climb out the chimney. What do you think of that answer?" (This had indeed been suggested by some children who did not know the riddle.)

The children's responses may be classified as follows. (a) In one group there was no apparent acknowledgment of joke conventions, no differentiation between joking and nonjoking answers. The predominant motive was to give an answer to a question, to find a way out of a problem situation. Magical, punning, or materially feasible means were equally acceptable. (b) A child would reject nonjoking expedients as not funny, but might then become so carried away by the problem situation that he would discuss such solutions from the point of view of practicability, dropping the consideration of joke conventions. (c) A child attempts to exclude nonjoking solutions by so delimiting the imagined situation that no practical expedient is possible. (This maneuver cannot be applied to all jokes; it depends on the kind of situation the joke deals with.) (d) The child rejects nonjoking alternatives as inappropriate to a joke or a riddle.

Let us consider these various reactions in more detail. In the first group we find children who did not know the answer and gave nonjoking answers as well as those who oscillated between joking and nonjoking answers without distinguishing between them. Six-year-old Doris with whom I have already discussed jokes at some length does not know the riddle. She proposes: "Break the window to get out. Or if he had very hard furniture, bang the door open. Climb out the chimney." Eight-year-old Tony says: "He smashes the windows and gets out. Are the windows locked? . . . Or he opens up the roof. Is the roof locked too? Are the walls locked? He just sits in bed reading the calendar and eating an apple. What's the answer?" Ten-year-old Hilda, who also does not know the riddle, says: "He bangs—no, he can climb through the chimney. Break the windows open, dig a hole, go through the cellar." "Is that a joke answer?" "He could dig a hole in the wall." "Is that funny?" "Not too much, but anyone who digs a hole in the wall is really crazy." Thus she attempts to meet the demand for a joke by saying that the behavior she describes would be sufficiently wild and crazy to be funny. Possibly Doris and Tony also thought that their solutions had a funny quality because of the violence of the actions they suggested.

Frequently in this first group, we find children who know the joking answer but shift without apparent awareness of the discrepancy to a non-joking alternative. Eight-year-old Frank knows one of the stock answers: "He played baseball and if he got an out he'd be outside." However, he adds: "I'd get out because my house has screws and I have a screwdriver to fit." Eight-year-old Judy says: "He played the piano till he found the right key. . . . He might take a long stick and push it under the door and hold it by the very end." She attempts to describe how the outside lock on the door might be unfastened in this way. Turning to the question of how to live in the locked house, she says: "And there wasn't any food? If there was a sink and water, that wouldn't keep him alive. . . ."

Nine-year-old Denis is very much taken up with this problem; as he tells me later his mother locks him in his room when he is bad. He appears to accept joking and nonjoking alternatives as equivalent ways out. First he asks: "Did he have anything with him? Was he dressed? Did he have a belt? He could take the belt buckle and unlock the door." I then tell him the piano solution; Denis inquires what else the man has, and I say a bed and a calendar. He reasons: "And he has a piano. And he's living and dressed. He could take the springs from the bed and have water. But you can't live just on water. Of course we know he could get out whenever he wants to because he has the piano and he has his belt." Thus Denis throws together the possibilities picking a lock with a belt buckle and using a piano key. He goes on to describe an "old cowboy trick" for getting out of a locked room when the key is on the outside of the door. He uses a similar device "when my mother locks me in my room when I'm bad."

Eight-year-old Walter ranges from punning to realistic to magical solutions: "He had a piano and he kept on playing till he got the right key. . . . He could stick his head out the window and call for help. There's one about a man in a tower with twenty-five cents with an eagle on it. So he woke up the eagle and it flew him out." Of course the use of the piano key to open the door may also be understood by the children in a realistic sense. Several of them have literal images of yanking the key off the piano and discuss whether this could be done or not.

When the children who do not know the riddle give non-joking answers they would seem to be motivated by wanting to answer at all costs.[64] In young children the wish to answer overpowers the requirement to abide by certain rules, as here the rules of joke construction. When pressed for an answer they easily pass over these boundaries, which are in any case not very firmly established. This is analogous to their resorting to a magical way out when pressed on a practical question to which they cannot find a solution. What is more puzzling, however, is their readiness to accept the suggestion of climbing up the chimney when I propose it following the joking answers. A number of children rejected the chimney solution not on the grounds of its violation of joke conventions, but on material grounds, raising difficulties as to how one could get a toe-hold inside a chimney, etc. Here it would seem that the dividing line between joking and nonjoking discourse is weakly established—especially in the case of an imaginary situation which is emotionally so compelling. The child follows the suggestion to shift from joking to nonjoking expedients without demur because he feels little sense of discrepancy. The point is to multiply solutions in an effort to reduce the anxiety aroused by the imaginary situation and he is not choosy about means. It may be thought that the child complies to a suggestion of the adult without wanting to criticize it. But we shall see

that children who have grasped the joke conventions repudiate the suggestion. In any case the children were not
inclined to accept the chimney solution; what varied were
the grounds for their rejection.

Six-year-old Robbie tells a variant which he knows of
the locked house riddle: "A man lost his key and the door
was locked and he couldn't open any of the windows. How
did he get in?—He ran around until he was all in." I tell
him about the man locked in with the calendar, bed and
piano. Robbie is able with a few hints to supply the punning answers. I then asked him if the man could climb up
the chimney—could that be an answer? He says: "No,
because how could he climb up the chimney?" "What's
the difference between taking a key from the piano and
climbing up the chimney?" "He couldn't get up the chimney anyhow. Because maybe he'd be able to yank a key off
the piano." Seven-year-old Norbert says appreciatively
when I tell him this joke: "That's a good one," laughing
particularly at the water from the springs in the bed. However, when I ask what he thinks of the chimney solution,
he says: "I don't know. Because there's always a little
thing on the top like a strainer. It could be locked so he
couldn't get out. It could have a padlock on it."

A thirteen-year-old boy protests at the suggestion of
the chimney solution: "How could he climb up? It's impossible." He tries to think how one could get a hand- or
toe-hold. Similarly, a thirteen-year-old girl objects: "How
could he get off the roof? And how could he climb up?
Unless he took some bricks out. . . ."

Let us now turn to the second group in which there is
an awareness of the discrepancy between joking and nonjoking discourse but where the division is still not firmly
established. Six-year-old John laughs when I tell him the
locked house joke and asks admiringly: "Who thought

that up? I couldn't think that up." He then goes over to the outside door of the room we are in and tries it: "Hey, we could get out of this place. We're not locked in." Despite this association in terms of a real predicament, he is able to criticize a realistic answer to the joke as inappropriate. When I propose the chimney solution he says: "It wouldn't be a funny answer. The other answer was funny." "What's the difference?" "There are no such things as keys to open doors on a piano, no such things as dates you can eat on a calendar, no such things called springs on a bed." Thus he seems to have grasped that the funny solutions are not real solutions at all. However, he then goes on to the same criticism of the chimney which we have heard from the other children: "Anyhow how could he climb up the chimney? Unless he had sharp toes to stick in the cement . . . or something to drill holes."

In the next group, we find a rejection of the nonjoking answer, but not yet on the grounds of pure joke convention. The children attempt to qualify the imaginary situation in such a way that nonjoking answers will be excluded. Ten-year-old Jed says to the chimney solution: "It wouldn't be a joke. By the way, you should say there's no chimneys or anything. That's part of the joke." Similarly, eleven-year-old Stephen explains in the same connection: "You have to go through a lot of gimmicks— walls ten feet thick, no windows, no door, no chimney."

In the last group, we find children who repudiate nonjoking answers entirely on the grounds that they are not funny, that it would not be a joke. Nine-year-old Fred knows many variants of the locked house: "What does he have in it? If he has a baseball and bat—three strikes and you're out. If he's outside, he ran around till he was all in. He can play the piano till he finds the right key. He can get out of a church because it's holy." "How about climb-

ing out the chimney?" Fred says scornfully: "Does that
sound like a riddle to you? It's not a joke!" Eleven-year-
old Jack has not heard the joke before and laughs when
I tell it. When I propose the chimney, he says: "No,
cause you didn't say there was a chimney." "Suppose
there was." "That's different. But it wouldn't be a funny
answer. People have been known to climb out chimneys."
Similarly ten-year-old Peter says: "Climbing up the chimney you really could do. The piano keys are funny because it's something that couldn't happen—a word that's
spelled the same way but doesn't mean the same." Twelve-
year-old Laura says of the chimney: "There's no pun.
It's something a person could have done." Thirteen-year-
old Nicholas says that whoever gave the chimney answer
"shouldn't become a comedian. The answer is not in terms
of the joke, but how he would get out of there."

Some children who were sufficiently subtle about joke
conventions remarked that the chimney solution reminded
them of the riddles about the fireman's suspenders and
the chicken crossing the road, where the answers are unexpectedly expected; the hearer anticipates a trick and is
told something obvious. Eleven-year-old Dorothy says of
the chimney: "It's not a very good one. There's a series
of riddles that have sensible answers—Why did the chicken
cross the road? Why does Uncle Sam wear red, white, and
blue suspenders? Why does the fireman wear a red hat?
There people try to find a pun. Sometimes in pun riddles,
they give sensible answers and there it's wrong." Similarly
eleven-year-old Stephen says of the chimney solution:
"It's as silly as 'Why did the chicken cross the road?'"

III

While joke comprehension tends to increase with age,
there are other important factors to which it is related.

Intelligence and interest in jokes are both relevant. The rules of correct joke construction are something the child has to learn. Other things being equal, the child of good intelligence who generally learns easily will also master with greater facility the modes of joke formation. Dull children or those retarded in learning are slower to grasp the rules implicit in jokes. But motivation is also a major determinant. The child who has found in joking a particularly valuable device for solving emotional difficulties, or for expressing otherwise unacceptable impulses, is apt to gain a quicker mastery of joke technique. Six-year-old John, who was able to distinguish better than many much older children between a joking and nonjoking answer, was exceptionally interested in telling and inventing jokes. Throughout the year that I visited his class he was intensely eager to tell me jokes, of which he had a large, varied, and constantly growing repertoire. When I asked one of the girls in his class where she had learned the jokes she told me, she said, "That John! He knows so many and tells so many."

Nine-year-old Fred, who was so scornful of the nonjoking answer ("Does that sound like a riddle to you? It's not a joke!") has mastered joke conventions better than many children considerably older than he. He combines superior intelligence with an intense interest in jokes. Thus he collects numerous variants of the same joke and improvises additions of his own. Fred has found in jokes a permissible way of expressing hostile impulses which he has had great difficulty in mastering. He has been destructive toward other children and rebellious against authority. A major theme of his preferred jokes is mockery of authority figures. This was already noticeable in jokes he told me when he was seven, and has increased with time. He uses his good intelligence to show

up the weaknesses of the adults, and finds in the adoption
of joke conventions a way of making his attacks socially
acceptable. By adhering to precise rules he tries to bring
his hostility under control. These rules have the further
virtue that they can be turned against others. He can be
contemptuous of anyone who does not catch on. On the
basis of his mastery of joke conventions he could be
sharply critical of me when I proposed a violation of them.

Denis, who is the same age as Fred, but who does not
distinguish between the belt buckle and the piano key as
devices for unlocking the door, is less intelligent and also
suffers from a learning disturbance. This would seem to
have affected his grasp of joke conventions along with
other items of learning. We should keep in mind that we
are dealing here with verbal wit, the most intellectual
form of joking. A child's skill in it is not necessarily the
same as in more diffuse humorous or comic modes of expression. Thus Denis, whose mastery of word play is
slight, nevertheless maintains a humorous tone in talking
with me and turns happenings from the life of his family
into comic anecdotes. Fred, on the other hand, has a rather
severe pedantic manner and discusses jokes with the air
of a connoisseur. There is no doubt that he enjoys his
jokes, especially where they degrade authority figures,
but he seems more bound to the rigorous joke form and
less free in general joking talk.

Joke comprehension varies not only with age, intelligence, and interest in jokes, but also with the particular
joke, its technical ease or difficulty and its theme. The
locked house riddle was especially difficult both because
the clues to the punning answers were far from patent
and because of the strong feelings mobilized by its latent
meanings. Many children who offered nonjoking answers
to this one were able to produce joking answers to riddles

which were more obvious or less disturbing. Here is an instance where disturbing connotations overpowered the tendency to joke in a child with good facility for verbal wit. Ten-year-old Alfred is highly intelligent and very fond of joking. One day we were asking each other riddles out of a book. I presented him with the following: "Why didn't the moron need glasses?" Alfred answered: "Because he had perfect vision?" (Correct answer: Because he always drank out of the bottle.) Some time later I asked Alfred the same riddle. He had forgotten the answer and guessed: "Because he couldn't see?" Thus his anxiety about physical intactness or defect prevented him from reacting to this riddle in a joking manner. The first answer was a denial of the fear which broke through on the second occasion: perhaps the moron was blind.

IV

Where a joke is less disturbing in content or simpler in technique, it is easier for children to respond to it appropriately. We can observe the same sequence in their reactions, from ignoring the joke conventions, to vacillating about them, to maintaining them in a clear-cut way. But the latter stages appear at an earlier age. There is no one moment when joke conventions are mastered. This varies with the occasion and the topic of the joke, as well as the capacities and motivations of the individual child. Let us consider the children's responses to another joke: Why did the moron take the ladder to school?—Because he wanted to get into a higher grade. Or, because he wanted to go to high school. This was easier for the children than the locked house, partly because the situation involved less intense feelings, partly because the key word "high," with its associations of intellectual ambition seemed to come readily to mind. Again I submitted to the children an al-

ternative nonjoking answer which one child had given me:
Because he wanted to climb out the window.

Here are, first, children who fail to observe the joke
conventions. Six-year-old Donald, who does not know this
riddle, says: "Because he wanted to climb up the ladder
I suppose. It's not so reasonable." Six-year-old Doris
guesses: "Because he wanted to get into school earlier?"
After I have told nine-year-old Maggy the answer, I ask
her if she could think of another one. She says: "To climb
the monkey-bars maybe, instead of using the monkey
bars."

Ten-year-old Hilda says: "I think I heard it. Oi weh!
I should remember. Cause he wanted to climb in the window?" When I tell her the answer she laughs and says:
"That's really crazy. He'd have to go to school and learn
multiplication. . . . So there's no sense in trying to get
into a higher grade." This exemplifies a common criticism
of jokes on the part of children who have not grasped
joke conventions. They object that the joking answer is
"crazy" or "silly" or "doesn't make sense" or that you
"can't really do that." As we have seen, children who
have a better understanding of joke conventions may distinguish the joking solution as something that could not
actually be done. Eight-year-old Betty criticizes the joke
in the same way that Hilda has done: "Oh, I think that's
silly, because you can't really do that."

In an intermediate stage a child proposes nonjoking
answers, but then becomes aware of their inappropriateness. Eight-year-old Louise says: "I think it has something to do with school work." I tell her the answer and
then ask if she can think of any others. She says: "No,
unless he was a little midget and the teacher asked him to
do sums on the blackboard and he couldn't reach up. Or
she put the sums at the top of the board." Louise seems to

be thinking quite literally of the possible uses of a ladder in school. She gives us an image of the child's aspirations and sense of inadequacy; she feels like a "little midget" who finds the problems the teacher gives over her head. Thus she expresses the idea of intellectual heights in visual imagery rather than in word play. She then proceeds to criticize what she has said: "But some of these riddles you have to have a joke answer."

Seven-year-old Marcia is able to give a joking answer which appears to be an original variant on the usual ones: "Because he wanted to get high in arithmetic? I just figured it out." When I tell her that he wanted to get to a higher grade, she protests: "But he can't with a ladder. The moron is somebody who's crazy." She seems uncertain whether the impossibility is a ground for criticizing the joke or is definitive of it. Nell, also seven, seems inclined to the latter alternative. When I tell her the answer she says: "That's a funny one. Know why? Because you can't get to a higher grade. . . . You can't climb up to it." Similarly ten-year-old Betsy, after giving the answer, "to climb to a higher grade," explains why it is funny: "Because no one could climb to a higher grade. You have to work to get to a higher grade."

Older children improvised freely on this theme. "Maybe how to get up in the world" (twelve-year-old girl). "He wanted to step up on his grades" (twelve-year-old boy). "To climb to success" (thirteen-year-old girl). "To climb the ladder of success" (thirteen-year-old boy). "To be ahead . . . a head taller than everyone" (thirteen-year-old girl).

In response to the climbing out the window alternative, eleven-year-old Dorothy says: "It isn't okay because it isn't a pun." Eleven-year-old Stephen remarks: "It's not the answer for a riddle, it's just ordinary." Fourteen-year-old Elton distinguishes the window answer from his own "ladder of success": "One is trying to be funny—the other is logical." Thus eventually what is logical, sensible, or literally feasible gets rejected as not meeting the requirements of the joke. Twelve-year-old Laura says of whoever proposed the window answer: "They weren't thinking very hard. . . . It's not a moron joke if it's put that way. . . . It doesn't fit the tradition of the moron jokes. . . . It's supposed to be a moronic answer."

The distinction between joking and nonjoking discourse is thus established gradually. That joking has its own rules which run counter to those of reasonable thought is often bewildering to younger children. They may object to a joke as not making sense, trying to maintain their hold on reality. Older children understand that it is the nonsensical which makes sense in terms of the joke. We have seen how the children strive to express their growing awareness of these two opposite ways of making sense. By the beginning of adolescence intelligent children seem to have grasped that in the sphere of the joke the nonsensical is not only permitted but required. We may infer that up until this age children are frequently uncertain how to take jokes; they are struggling with the effort to make sense in reasonable, realistic terms. We have also seen how much the ability to shift to the nonsensical varies with the topic of the joke and the kind and intensity of emotion it arouses.

Conclusion

THERE are two ways of looking at children. In one way they are very different from adults; in another way they are much alike. The style of joking, the concentration on certain themes, the mastery of joke conventions vary with age. But the underlying motive of joking, to transform painful and frustrating experiences and to extract pleasure from them, is the same throughout. The mockery of the grown-ups who are so powerful, enviable, and morally forbidding (but are they really so good themselves?) persists in adult jokes which show the fallible side of authority figures. The sexual exposure of the withholding mother, in the jokes about the mother with the little boy called Heinie (where the mother is always going around asking, "Have you seen my Heinie?"), exemplifies a motive common to all sexual joking: to override restrictions and gain the withheld gratification in spite of them. Jokes achieve this in a different way from wish-fulfilment fantasies or fairy tales. There is an element of renunciation in joking, a mockery of the frustrated wishes themselves. The prerogatives of the envied grown-ups appear in a ridiculous light; the desired woman becomes an absurd figure; the urgent mystery (as, for instance, of the locked

house) is not really solved—a punning answer brushes
the question aside. In joking there is relief from the pressure of impulses, of sex, ambition, hostility, curiosity, and
a compensation for the painful dissatisfaction of all these
motives. In the elation that comes with laughter, the momentary sense of invulnerability, there is the feeling: how
little it all matters.

Freud considered that the motive of overcoming painful
feelings was peculiar to a special group of jokes, which he
called humorous, as distinct from the comic and the witty.
His key example was that of the criminal who was being
led to execution on a Monday morning and who remarked:
"Well, this is a good beginning for the week." [65] There
is in this a pretended comic error of thought in that the
condemned man seems to overlook the fact that he has no
week to look forward to. But in thus denying the crucial
difference for him between this Monday and any other
Monday he wards off overwhelmingly painful feelings.
For the bystanders similarly there is a pleasurable shift
of emotion: they can laugh instead of feeling pity. In
such an instance the relation of the joke to the painful
situation which it aims to master is explicit. I should like
to suggest that what distinguishes such humor from other
occasions of joking may be just the explicitness of the
connection with the painful experience behind it. In other
cases the source of the joke may be much less evident; the
lines of connection between the joke and the painful experiences which it rectifies may be more extended and
circuitous, and the joke teller and his hearers may not
be conscious of these connections.

Freud says that in most of the examples of wit and the
comic which he analyzes information about the motives of
their originators was lacking. However, he gives one instance where it was possible, from biographical material,

to trace the genesis of a witticism. A character, Hirsch-Hyacinth, in a story of Heine's, boasts after having attended a fine dinner: "I was sitting next to Solomon Rothschild and he treated me just as an equal, quite famillionaire." That is, Rothschild treated this insignificant man as familiarly as was compatible with his being a millionaire. The comic character in Heine's story, as Freud points out, bears some resemblance to Heine himself. Just as this character changed his name from Hirsch to Hyacinth, so Heine had changed his first name from Harry to Heinrich. Heine had been treated very condescendingly by rich relatives. "We know from many a record how keenly Heine suffered from these repulses at the hands of his wealthy relatives in his youth and during later years. The witticism 'famillionaire' grew out of the soil of such a subjective feeling." [66]

The difference between Heine's "famillionaire" joke and the humor of the condemned man lies in the more extended and elaborate route between the painful experience and the joke which transforms it. With most jokes this relation to their source remains hidden. But I would suggest that where this concealed genesis can be uncovered it is likely that the same process will be found at work. In the joking of children I have tried to show, sometimes in terms of the predicament of an individual child (as with the little boy who turns into a joke his anxious waiting all alone after school), sometimes in terms of the characteristic exigencies of a particular phase of development (as in the joking riddles of latency period children), how the underlying motive of the joke is to transform painful experiences. And this applies equally to the originator of a joke and to the one who finds and retells a ready-made joke which suits his own emotional needs.

Adults are apt to find children's jokes unfunny partly

because of differences in technical expertise, partly because the adult and the child rarely find themselves in the same emotional situation at the same time. However, if we can put ourselves in the child's place, we can see that his motives for joking are not different from our own.

Children go through a two-sided development in relation to joking: they progressively incorporate inhibitions against the simple expression of impulses, and they progressively master technical devices by means of which these inhibitions can be circumvented. But adulthood is not defined by exclusive adherence to the most advanced phase of this progression. Under favorable circumstances, of an elated mood, good company, good drink, special intimacy, the most childish forms of joking become again accessible.[67] Slapstick comedy and sheer bawdiness may delight those who can also appreciate the most refined wit. The range widens with age, but ideally to the adult the whole range is open. Children are not so remote from us. If we cannot always laugh with them, we can at times laugh like them.

Appendix: On Data

IN TRYING to find out what children consider funny my main procedure was to interview children individually. I had at first wanted to observe spontaneous joking, clowning and laughter in group situations, but I discovered that with children of seven and over the best jokes are apt to be whispered. While I continued with group observations, especially of children under seven, I began to concentrate on individual interviews, where I found most of the children eagerly communicative. I told children of four and five that I wondered if they could tell me a funny story; children of six to about nine, that I was making a book of jokes and funny stories for children and that I would appreciate their telling me some they liked; and older children that I was investigating what children consider funny at different ages. I asked them to tell me jokes they knew, funny things that had happened in class, things that had made them laugh; from whom they had learned their jokes; whether they had made up some themselves; whether they could make up a funny story or draw me a funny picture; whether they could recall funny things from movies or television. I asked them if they had brothers or sisters and tried to find out what differences there were between jokes they liked and those preferred by younger or older siblings; also what things the child used to think funny that he now rejected. I inquired what kinds of jokes their parents made and whether the children thought them funny. The questions about what was funny were interspersed in a rather free-flowing conversation in which I encouraged the child to talk about his family, his teacher, his classmates, the children on the block or whatever else he seemed inclined to chat about. In this way spontaneous reminiscences were evoked in the course of which the child might recall family jokes; a boy told how he and his mother made up riddles together; another boy told how he made his little brother laugh to divert him from crying after a fight; a girl told what she and her sister laughed about after they were in bed at night, and so on. Thus the children supplied not only jokes they knew but often also some of the context and atmosphere of their joking.

My subjects in these interviews were ninety children in a New York City private school. The children were between the ages of four and twelve inclusive, ten from each age group, five boys and five girls. Most of the children were interviewed once, but occasionally a child might be interviewed two or three times. With children of four and five, whom I visited frequently in class, I was able to record funny stories they made up off and on over the period of a school year. This interview material was supplemented, as I have said, by observations in the class room (this included also three-year-olds), and by information provided by teachers. I consulted the school record of each child I interviewed, which included detailed observations of behavior, accounts of home visits and interviews with parents, as well as reports of school achievement. In addition I drew on more intensive observations of children who were in treatment with me for learning difficulties. Where there was the opportunity I have observed and talked with children more informally, and I have drawn on reports which parents have given me.

As my first series of interviews left some questions about children's comprehension of jokes and about possibly suppressed associations (where the joke sounded very harmless but I suspected the children might have some other ideas about it), I proceeded to a second series of interviews to investigate these points. Here instead of asking the children to tell me jokes, I told them that I would tell them some which I had heard to see whether they liked them. I tried to see whether the child could tell me why it was funny or not funny, whether he understood the terms involved, what he thought about the motivations of the joke protagonist, and whether (in the case of joking riddles) he could think of alternative answers. I also took this occasion to ask the children to define some key terms, such as "riddle," "moron," and "joke." In this series of interviews I started with children of six and went up to seventeen-year-olds, since I found that at twelve and thirteen there were still children whose understanding of joke conventions and technique remained incomplete. In this second series I interviewed fifty-five children (13 six- and seven-year-olds, 15 eight- and nine-year-olds, 12 ten- through twelve-year-olds, and 15 thirteen- through seventeen-year-olds; for the latter age group I drew on a second New York City private school, similar to the first). Working downwards in the age scale, I tried out in conversations with four- and five-year-olds some of the jokes I had heard from older children to see whether they would understand them and what they would make of them.

Since my main data are from interviews I have more information about verbal joking than about clowning and comic acting. Also my observations concentrated more on the activity of making and telling jokes than on chance occurrences that occasion laughter. My direct observations of children's joking and laughing together were, as I have said, more limited than the information the children gave me about these things. One may suspect that the children were somewhat selective in what they reported to an adult. However, in the school where I made this study the atmosphere was fairly free, and I got the impression that the children were inclined to speak with some candor. A considerable number, for instance, told me dirty jokes. Their communicativeness, however, varied with age. Children up to ten seemed to delight in the opportunity for displaying their repertoire of jokes. After this age there was an increasing tendency to be secretive and guarded towards the adult. I should add that on several occasions I interviewed two children together which made it possible to observe some of the joking and teasing by-play between them.

The children I studied were from urban, mainly professional, mainly Jewish families, and their school was a progressive private school. They were mostly above average intelligence and highly developed in verbal skills. As the group was fairly homogeneous in these respects it provided a favorable basis for observing age differences. However, other studies would be needed to determine whether the same kinds of jokes are told among children of different groups in our society, to see what the effects might be, for instance, of a less sophisticated and less tolerant environment or one which placed less value on verbal expertise. A collaborator of mine, Mrs. Lucy Toma, interviewed a small sample of middle-class public school children in a town in Kansas (eighteen children between the ages of six and ten) using the questions of my first series of interviews. The results were similar to those from children of the same ages whom I interviewed; there was, for instance, the same interest in joking riddles which I had found so prominent in school age children, and some of the jokes were identical for the two groups. Jokes are notably ephemeral, although I found that the children I talked with told some of the same jokes I had heard in my childhood. It would be a subject for further study at some later date to see what jokes will replace those now popular with children, whether the changes will be in content or in form as well.

Notes

1. Freud has shown that the intention of imputing nonsense to another person is a frequent motive for the use of nonsense in jokes. *Wit and Its Relation to the Unconscious.*

2. Freud has interpreted nonsense in dreams about the dead father as expressing ambivalence: I did and did not want him to die. *The Interpretation of Dreams.*

3. Cf. Freud's analysis of the comic effect of errors of thought in *Wit and Its Relation to the Unconscious.*

4. Bertram D. Lewin, *The Psychoanalysis of Elation.*

5. This appeared in an exhibition of paintings of French children, 13 to 16, at the Museum of Modern Art in New York in the spring of 1948.

6. In her clinical papers on humor, Lucile Dooley observed how patients produced humorous fantasies specifically in connection with working through their oedipal disappointments. In such a context a woman patient imagined, for instance, that she was a tiny ant that was going to be crushed by her huge father; she felt this to be funny. ("A Note on Humor," *Psychoanalytic Review,* 1934.) A man patient conjured up an image of himself as a small boy in a high chair being fed by his mother, and found it pathetic but also amusing that the little fellow did not realize that he was going to be gypped. ("The Relation of Humor to Masochism," *Psychoanalytic Review,* 1941.) Dooley calls these "proto-humorous" productions, expressing a humorous attitude but lacking the elaboration which would make them communicable jokes. She explains the occurrence of these humorous feelings at the time when oedipal disappointments are being worked through on the assumption that humor is intimately involved with the super-ego, which emerges out of oedipal renunciations.

7. Melanie Klein has observed that young children often react to parental intercourse, or their fantasies about it, by wetting and soiling, which they imagine as destructive acts towards the parents. *The Psychoanalysis of Children.*

8. Ernest Jones, "The Phantasy of the Reversal of Generations," *Papers on Psychoanalysis.*

9. Freud has pointed out the relation of comic contrasts of large and small to the size discrepancies of children and adults. (*Wit and Its Relation to the Unconscious*). Dooley indicates another basic instance of size discrepancy, the contrast between the clitoris and the penis. ("The Relation of Humor to Masochism," *Psychoanalytic Review*, 1941.) Some of the formulations of earlier theorists on humor would seem to refer, though without the authors' conscious awareness, to this latter discrepancy. Thus Herbert Spencer defined the ludicrous in terms of a "descending incongruity," an effect produced when we expect something great but find something small instead. ("Physiology of Laughter," *Essays Scientific, Political and Speculative,* vol. 2). Kant's definition of the comic may be interpreted as a more extreme view of the sex difference, not of large and small, but as somthing and nothing. He finds that the characteristic situation in which laughter occurs is one in which strained expectation is suddenly transformed into nothing. (*Critique of Judgment.*)

10. Paul Schilder, "Psychoanalytic Remarks on Alice in Wonderland and Lewis Carroll," *Journal of Nervous and Mental Disease*, 1938; Martin Grotjahn, "About the Symbolization of Alice's Adventures in Wonderland," *American Imago*, 1947; John Skinner, "Lewis Carroll's Adventures in Wonderland," *The Yearbook of Psychoanalysis*, 1948; Otto Fenichel, "The Symbolic Equation: Girl = Phallus," *The Psychoanalytic Quarterly*, 1949.

11. Bertram D. Lewin has observed that "nothing" frequently refers to the female genital. "The Nature of Reality, the Meaning of Nothing, with an Addendum on Concentration," *The Psychoanalytic Quarterly*, 1948.

12. Theodore Huff, *Charlie Chaplin.*

13. Freud, "Humour," *Collected Papers*, vol. 5.

14. Freud has emphasized that we contrast the way we would behave with the actions of the comic personage; also that the person who appears unperturbed at his own misfortune saves us the expenditure of sympathetic distress. *Wit and Its Relation to the Unconscious.*

15. G. Berguer, "La Puissance du Nom, ses Origines Psychologiques," *Archives de Psychologie*, 1936.

16. Ernst Kris, "Ego Development and the Comic," *Psychoanalytic Explorations in Art.*

17. Lucile Dooley describes a patient, a 42-year-old man, who had an exceptionally intense interest in word play jokes, and who apparently retained good contact with their infantile sources. He was fond of joking with small children in this way. He would hail a little girl with, "Good morning, Big Boy," and was delighted if the child would retort, "Hello, Little Lady." The theme of sex difference was also a frequent one in his more sophisticated jokes. ("The Relation of Humor to Masochism," *Psychoanalytic Review*, 1941.)

18. Genesis, Chapter 17.

19. Lewis Carroll, "The Hunting of the Snark," Fit the First.

20. Similarly feelings about a particular theme of fantasy vary de-

pending on whether it finds expression in the mythology of the culture. Hindu mythology includes numerous fantasies in which a hero is incorporated by a huge divine personage and wanders through the interior of his body. (cf. Heinrich Zimmer, *The King and the Corpse*.) In western culture there is not a similar acceptance of such fantasies; they do not find a noticable place among the wonders of fairy tale and folk lore. Thus even quite young children, in whom such fantasies are common, tend to regard them as funny. A four-year-old girl presents the following as a funny story: "Instead of a school building there was a school person. And it could walk away. And it couldn't sit at the table. . . . Once there was a lady apple and she didn't want to eat any food. She ate paint brushes and boards. And once she ate a whole school up and ate all the children up. And you know what? The apple lady didn't want to eat anything next day. She never wanted to eat anything. She was a tiny baby and she went to school. She was only so big, and then she got this big."

21. Ernst Kris and E. H. Gombrich, "The Principles of Caricature," in Ernst Kris' *Psychoanalytic Explorations in Art.*

22. Piaget, *The Child's Conception of the World.*

23. Freud, *Wit and Its Relation to the Unconscious.*

24. In a case analyzed by Annie Reich, a woman with a strong drive towards comic acting repeatedly portrayed foolish and ugly women with the intention of showing how repulsive her mother and sisters were. ("The Structure of the Grotesque-Comic Sublimation," *Bulletin of the Menninger Clinic,* 1949.)

25. Louisa Düss describes how a 22-year-old psychotic woman reestablished her sense of her own identity by recapitulating the learning of her own name. First out of a stream of meaningless sounds she produced "mon enfant," which she repeated in alternately loving and hostile tones, assuming the rôle of her mother towards her infantile self. Subsequently she recovered her name, in the saying of which she became the child, naming herself, and possessed of a separate identity from the mother. In speaking her own name in a loving tone, she also incorporated the affectionate mother. ("The Psychological Function of the Proper Name in the Reconstruction of the Personality of a Schizophrenic," *Psychiatric Quarterly,* 1948.)

26. Freud has analyzed dirty jokes as a means of exposing a woman against her will. (*Wit and Its Relation to the Unconscious.*)

27. Freud finds the comic of self-exposure an instance of too little expenditure of mental effort. (*Ibid.*)

28. Otto Fenichel, "The Misapprehended Oracle," *American Imago,* 1942. Children achieve a mocking compliance by shifting the meaning of adult's words so that a prohibition becomes a permission. For instance, a little boy, told not to play with himself "down there," gets into a position where his genitals are higher than his head to masturbate.

29. These generalizations are based on New York City private school children. In less clever and sophisticated groups, the age of acquisition and of abandonment of riddles might well be later.

30. Geza Roheim, *The Riddle of the Sphinx*. As an alternative to Roheim's interpretation, three legs may represent the father (the penis appearing as the third leg) ; two legs, the mother; four legs, the couple joined together.

31. Riddling is the counterpart in myth and fairy tale of epistemological rationalism. Rationalism, in which the aim is to achieve knowledge by pure thought, is motivated by the wish to avoid the hazards of empirical investigation. The Oedipus myth implies that such avoidance is not possible. In contrast to this, fairy tales, in which the riddler can know without looking, grant the wish of the rationalist, along with other impossible wishes.

32. Piaget has observed how children deny having learned the rules of games they know and believe they have found them in their heads. *The Moral Judgment of the Child.*

33. Plato, with his abhorrence of the act of procreation, believed that the archetypes of all our ideas have existed eternally.

34. Freud, *Wit and Its Relation to the Unconscious.*

35. Martin Grotjahn, "The Inability to Remember Dreams and Jokes," *Psychoanalytic Quarterly*, 1951.

36. For children in the past, or in less urban surroundings, the hazards of the chicken's excursion may have been imagined in other terms.

37. Freud, *The Interpretation of Dreams.*

38. Roheim observes that riddles about numbers of legs are frequent in folklore, as for instance the following of Finnish origin. "Two legs sat upon three legs eating one leg": a man on a stool eating a ham. The fascination of such riddles derives from the (often concealed) sexual associations of legs. *The Riddle of the Sphinx.*

39. Freud, "A Childhood Recollection from *Dichtung und Wahrheit,*" *Collected Papers*, vol. 4.

40. Melanie Klein, *The Psychoanalysis of Children.*

41. Karl Abraham, "The Narcissistic Evaluation of Excretory Processes in Dreams and Neurosis," *Selected Papers on Psychoanalysis.*

42. Freud, *Wit and Its Relation to the Unconscious.*

43. Berta Bornstein, "Clinical Notes on Child Analysis," *The Psychoanalytic Study of the Child*, vol. 1.

44. Ludwig Eidelberg has analyzed the kind of joke construction which involves paying in advance for a forbidden gratification. "A Contribution to the Study of Wit," *Studies in Psychoanalysis.*

45. Freud, *Wit and Its Relation to the Unconscious.*

46. In a study by Mary Hester, in which original funny stories were collected from children, the most repeated theme in those of the latency period was that of falling. "Variation in Sense of Humour according to Age and Mental Condition," Columbia University Master's Thesis, 1924. —In the traditional theoretical literature on laughter, falling would seem to be the most recurrently mentioned comic act.

47. Fenichel states that equilibrium sensations often become "the representatives of infantile sexuality in general." *The Psychoanalytic Theory of Neurosis.*

48. Martha Wolfenstein and Nathan Leites, *Movies, A Psychological Study.* That such falling is auspicious indicates that sex has lost some of the older Biblical connotations of falling.

49. Ernst Kris has remarked on the necessity of dissociating fantasy from masturbation for purposes of literary development. "Approaches to Art," *Psychoanalytic Explorations in Art.*

50. B. A. Botkin, *A Treasury of American Folklore.*

51. Freud, *op. cit.*

52. *Ibid.*

53. *Ibid.*

54. Wolfenstein and Leites, *Movies, A Psychological Study.* In American film comedies a recurrent figure is the comic onlooker who sees the worst in ambiguous but actually harmless situations. He mistakenly supposes that the virtuous young couple are carrying on an affair, that the chaste wife is unfaithful, etc. By seeing these naughty possibilities through his eyes and at the same time laughing at his mistake, the audience can enjoy the forbidden while disclaiming responsibility for it.

55. Ella Sharpe observed that when patients said, "I've wandered off the point and can't find it again," or "I see your point of view, but I don't take it in," the unconscious reference was to suckling experiences: the point was the nipple which had eluded the infant. "Psycho-physical Problems Revealed in Language: An Examination of Metaphor," *Collected Papers on Psychoanalysis.*

56. Elli Herzfeld and Franziska Prager, "Verständnis für Scherz und Komik beim Kinde," *Zeitschrift für angewandte Psychologie,* 1929.

57. The combination of arbitrariness as to the acceptable answer and rigorous precision in its verbal formulation, which we find in latency period riddling, has its counterpart in rote learning for which children in this period show such aptitude. They accept the task of learning what is prescribed without requiring reasons for it; the authority of the adults is the adequate sanction. Similarly, as Piaget has observed, children at this age accept the rules of games as unalterable, without understanding their rationale. (*The Moral Judgment of the Child.*) With the onset of adolescence there is a change in the attitude towards learning and rules. There is a gradually increasing resistance to learning what is required simply for that reason, and the demand that what is to be learned have some additional meaning for the individual. The adolescent feels more free to modify rules as he has grasped the underlying principles involved and can apply them for himself. Similarly in joking, the adolescent is much less apt than the latency period child to learn his jokes by rote. He gets the gist of a humorous anecdote and reproduces it in his own words. It may be added that while the preliminary gambits of the joke may be variously presented, it is usually necessary to repeat the gag line exactly; the dénouement admits of less variation than the part leading up to it. There would seem to be a parallel in this to foreplay and orgasm in love making.

58. Theodor Reik, *Nachdenkliche Heiterkeit.*

59. Sidney Colvin, *Keats.*

224　*Notes*

60. Bergson regards laughter as a rebuke to the individual who has fallen into mechanical automatism where he should assert his prerogative, as a living being, always to experience novelty. *Laughter.*

61. Kris has remarked on the double-edged character of comic. If it is not successful it becomes painful, as the hearer discerns the insufficiently masked aggression of the speaker. "The Psychology of Caricature," *Psychoanalytic Explorations in Art.*

62. Jean Piaget (*The Language and Thought of the Child*) has remarked how frequently children supply their own meanings without realizing that they have misunderstood.

63. "A Phase in the Development of Children's Sense of Humor," The *Psychoanalytic Study of the Child,* vol. 6.

64. Piaget, *op. cit.*

65. Freud, *Wit and Its Relation to the Unconscious.*

66. *Ibid.*

67. Ernst Kris, "Art and Regression," *Transactions of the New York Academy of Sciences,* VI, 1944.